Clocktower Books
San Diego

Dead Move:

Kate Morgan & The Haunting Mystery
of Coronado, Fifth Edition
128th Anniversary of her Death 1892-2020

By

John T. Cullen

~ 1892 Coronado, California ~
A True Crime and Ghost Legend Investigation

Clocktower Books, Publisher
P.O. Box 600973
Grantville Station
San Diego, California 92160-0973

www.clocktowerbooks.com—-editorial@clocktowerbooks.com

——◆•◆——————————————————————————◆•◆——

Reader Choices:

Dead Move—factual analysis (nonfiction—this book in hand, a stand-alone)

Lethal Journey—1892 gaslight thriller based on <u>Dead Move</u>—stand-alone

Coronado Mystery—both books together in a special double edition

Contents

Dedication

Carolyn and Andrew

As always

And to
Elizabeth 'Lizzie' Wyllie
(c1868-1892)
The quintessentially classic and tragic
Victorian Fallen Angel

Special Thanks to our intrepid, detail-oriented editor, Sarah Dawson, for a great job on every line of this manuscript. Any errors of spelling, usage, grammar, or the like are the author's fault. Contact Mrs. Dawson at **WordPlay Editing** by email at **sdawson@wordplayediting.com**. The editorial website is

www.wordplayediting.com.

Special thanks to 1SG Richard Agler, USMC-Ret. for invaluable information regarding hand guns, ballistics, and related issues about the gun found by the hand of the mysterious, violently deceased woman remembered as The Beautiful Stranger.

Brief 2020 Foreword

In publishing a new edition of this nonfiction book of historical analysis, I became concerned about a build-up of prefaces dating to at least three updated editions from 2009 to 2020. As a reader, I prefer to not be bogged down in excessive preambles, so I moved the prefaces to the rear of this new 2020 edition. You'll find them listed as Appendix A.

The information in those prefaces is not trivial, and makes for interesting reading. However, I am sure you'll prefer to leap right into the thick of things with the original Prolog.

The story of how this book got its title (*Dead Move*) is amusing in itself. While the book is a detailed, scholarly analysis based on true history, the title is a bit playful. In short: our dispatcher at the Transportation Department was promoted to a manager position with the Hotel itself. I didn't see him for a few weeks, and then bumped into him on the grassy concourse between our building and the main hotel with its red roofs and white sides. We greeted each other, and I asked light-heartedly, "So... have you learned about any new ghostly doings lately?"

He replied: "Oh yes, we just had a Dead Move last night."

"A Dead Move?" I was baffled. I had never heard the term before.

He told me: "You know that often guests, as they register at the main desk, ask to stay in Room 3327. If the room is vacant, we let them take it. But we always advise them that guests in the past have reported it to be very haunted. We warn them... and again last night, we got a terrified, breathless phone call from Room 3327... saying 'Get us out of here! Now!' We're ready for them, so we send bellmen and guards to escort them to a different part of the hotel, far from the haunted room where the Beautiful Stranger stayed before she died from that gunshot to the head in 1892. It's called a Dead Move in the hotel industry because we move the guests from one room to another, without checking them out and re-registering them."

Many prominent persons have gone through a Dead Move. For example, in 1983, a heavily armed and trained Secret Service agent assigned to guard hotel guest Vice-President George H.W. Bush had a sufficiently scary experience in the middle of the night, and asked to be moved. It's always "how soon can you get here?" and they are typically standing outside the room with their luggage, ready to be moved.

I told him: "Thanks! You just gave me the title for my book."

So now you know why the primary title is *Dead Move*. The book is full of juicy information like that, so please enjoy a good read! (JTC)

Prolog:

A True Story That Will Not Die

Ghost by Gaslight

The story you are about to read is true on two counts—as a mystery story, and as a ghost story. The real-life mystery story in 1892 became an instant national sensation, laced with beauty, passion, and hope—but also conspiracy, betrayal, and ultimately violent death. This mystery (murder or suicide?) spawned a famous ghost saga that has endured over a century. Whether or not you believe in ghosts, the story of the 'Beautiful Stranger' is a living piece of Hotel del Coronado lore—and even skeptics may at times get goose bumps.

To capture the atmosphere, it is worth dwelling a moment on how I came upon this story. Being an author, semi-retired from the computer systems development industry, and in search of some fresh experiences, I took a part-time job several years ago as a shuttle van driver with the Hotel del Coronado near San Diego.

The Hotel del Coronado (or the Hotel Del to local residents, sometimes just 'the Del') is an official U.S. National Landmark and a San Diego icon. It is usually portrayed on book covers, in all of its splendor, as a white Victorian lady with her famous brick-red roofs. It sits on the Peninsula of San Diego, on a Pacific Ocean beach in the City of Coronado, facing away from the City of San Diego.

The Pacific Ocean laps at sugar-white beaches, just a tennis ball's throw from the rear stairs where the Beautiful Stranger died—who became the famous ghost who is said to still haunt the great resort to this day. Visible along that shore, to the southeast, is the southwestern corner of the contiguous United States—including Imperial Beach and Nestor—before you reach Tijuana, Baja California del Norte, Mexico.

The weather in Coronado is usually balmy and sunny, as tall fan palms rustle in a slight breeze under clear blue skies. Visible to the west (the shore runs east-west at the Hotel Del) is the looming ridge of Point Cabrillo, which overlooks the San Diego Harbor entrance where the first Spanish expedition dropped anchor more than four centuries ago. The view from the barren, wind-blown site of his future hotel toward Point Cabrillo must have reminded mega-rich developer John Spreckels of gorgeous South Pacific beaches in Hawai'i, where his father owned vast sugar cane plantations. That was back in 1887, when Spreckels first visited San Diego and fell in love with the place. He would go on to own much of the area, and leave a lasting impression on its history.

Millions of visitors come to the area every year. But there is another side to the image—dark, atmospheric, spooky. As this book will show, John Spreckels was a key player in the mysterious events of Thanksgiving Week 1892 that led to the Beautiful Stranger's violent, mysterious death, and her incarnation as the hotel's most famous ghost.

My two years at the hotel were fascinating—new things to learn, nice people, great surroundings, interesting history, sunshine, fresh air, rustling palm trees, crashing surf...topped off by the fact that I believe I have solved a great mystery of the Hotel del Coronado: The legend of an unknown woman who died violently and mysteriously on the hotel's back steps during a huge sea storm; and of her ghost, which thousands of visitors and some staff claim to have seen. I personally have met a number of people who claim to have witnessed ghostly manifestations, though I myself can't make that claim. Then again, maybe I missed something. After all, if there is a ghost, it's clear that she would be trying to tell us something, and I unwittingly stepped into the role of oracle to deliver her message: She is not Kate Morgan, as is commonly thought, but a beautiful young woman who was betrayed and abandoned in the midst of a cruel blackmail conspiracy. Her name was Elizabeth 'Lizzie' Wyllie. Lizzie was pregnant when she took her life out of despair—a fallen Victorian angel, in the true sense and sentiment of that age. I will explain it all in this book.

On many an evening when business was slow, we drivers in our black suits would sit in our vans waiting for passengers, by turns either in the dark, starlit parking lot below, or under the softly gleaming coach lights around the front entrance of the hotel. A good deal of our traffic was taking guests to or from Lindbergh International Airport, ten miles away. The ride included an enjoyable two mile jaunt nearly 300 feet in the air across the Coronado Bay Bridge (another San Diego icon).

Another substantial part of our evening traffic was bringing guests to or from eating and entertainment venues in the Gaslamp Quarter of San Diego. This is a modern salvage and gentrification of the long-decaying Victorian city and its infamous red light district, through which Kate Morgan and her accomplices moved. Today's Gaslamp Quarter (Fourth to Sixth Avenues east-west, and K Street to Broadway north-south) was the heart of downtown San Diego in the 1890s, with the notorious Stingaree district partially overlapping to the south. The Stingaree, which was one of the most violent and dangerous red light districts on the West Coast, took its name from the stingrays that are common on San Diego area shores, and have a poisonous stinger that causes agonizing pain, and can (rarely) kill. The saying about the red light district was: "You get stung as badly in the Stingaree as in San Diego Bay."

On many nights during the winter months as I sat waiting in the van, fog would roll in off the Pacific Ocean, and a chill would run up and down my spine in the cold, damp air. Sometimes you could hear the booming of naval guns out at sea (the Navy's Special Warfare Command has its headquarters a block away, housing the Navy SEALs). On a breezy night, you could hear the clasps on the main flag pole banging as if shaken by a crazed spirit desperate for attention. There are always stray sounds of someone laughing, or people talking, and snatches of music, or even the distant night cargo train blaring as it slowly rumbles through downtown San Diego. For the most part, though, the atmosphere is softly lit and quiet. On some nights, a dense sea fog (marine layer) percolates silently among the streets, buildings, and palm trees of Coronado. On other nights the air is clear, and calm, smelling sweetly of night-blooming jasmine and other scents.

A strange, almost eerie silence descends around the Hotel Del with dusk, amid those jutting turrets and many-angled white walls that overlook pine trees and luscious lawns. In the winter months, it gets dark as early as 4:30 in the afternoon. Fog creeps up from the sea, and dampness brings with it a chill that crawls up your back and touches skeletal fingers along your spine. The valets and doormen stand about talking when things are slow. Some evenings are incredibly busy, and a constant stream of taxis and vans and cars presses through the narrow, circular driveway. Men and women in evening wear move leisurely up the front stairway and through the wide entrance.

On other evenings, the entrance has a ghostly calm about it—when the census is down, or during the interstice of the dinner hour, between the rush of arrivals and the rush of departures. A balmy glow of coach lamps bathes the area. Soft light in rich hues emanates from a large stained glass picture window above, which portrays the Amazon queen Califia (or Calafia) amid all the splendors of her realm. Calafia was, in a Spanish novel of 1510, a fictional queen ruling a mythical island named California, to be found on the route westward from Europe, which Christopher Columbus took in search of a sea passage to India. From this, our state derived its romantic name.

As you stand facing the hotel about 50 feet from the main entry, you see the curving windows of the Crown Room to your right. This contains a number of large chandeliers with light bulbs (high tech over a century ago) allegedly designed by L. Frank Baum, who often stayed at the Del after he published *The Wizard of Oz* in 1900. The Crown Room, at 23,500 square feet, is one of the largest all-wood halls of its kind in the United States. Its pine-vaulted ceiling is beautiful to behold, and has overarched the dinner table of many a president, king, movie star, and billionaire. The first royalty to dine in this room, in fact—and important to this book—was King David Kalakaua, the last King of Hawai'i, who came as a guest of John Spreckels for Christmas dinner in 1890, and died a few weeks later in San Francisco as a guest of Spreckels' Sugar Baron father, Claus Spreckels. John Spreckels, as we will see, was most likely the object of a blackmail conspiracy that puts the entire mystery of the 'Beautiful Stranger' in perspective. If Lizzie Wyllie is the key to the tragic mystery of the 'Beautiful Stranger,' the hotel's owner, John Spreckels, is the hinge upon which this tale turns.

One night, having gone to our office to warm up, I found a copy of the Heritage Department's beautifully written, illustrated, and designed book.[1] I started reading it in the Transportation Department's small office, upstairs in the same row of brick buildings as the original 1880s power plant. As I sat reading amid the odors of rotting carpets, decaying documents, and stale coffee, I was pretty quickly hooked on this captivating story. As is usually the case with history, it is amazing how much we actually know about the story—and yet, equally frustrating is the loss of information and artifacts that could help us resolve the many loose threads, baffling clues, and chilling dead ends.

The challenge I set myself was to see if I could figure out what really happened, using the copious details in the hotel's book and my own research at the library and online. Although I regaled thousands of visitors to San Diego with tales of the famous ghost—how the maids won't go in her room alone; how they go in to clean and make up beds in teams and get out as soon as possible; how a security officer I know was one of many people who have seen the outline of a Victorian woman on the bed, and if you smooth the blankets, the outline reappears as if by magic; how books fly off the shelves in the downstairs gallery; a whole set of ghostly doings like that—I was less interested in the

haunted aspect of the story as I was in the mystery of her life and violent death. All that follows grows out of my analysis of evidence that has been hidden in plain sight for well over a century. I offer many fine little points of reference and detail, most of which are important to the solution of the mystery, while a few will help visitors to the Hotel Del appreciate the history and local color of this national landmark.

&ed; &es;

Part I. Mystery Story

The Mystery in a Nutshell

Gunshot, by Gaslight, with Sea Storm and Ghost

On Thanksgiving Day, 1892, a beautiful and elegantly dressed young woman appeared at the Hotel del Coronado—the most luxurious resort in the region, whose doors had opened just a few years earlier in February 1888. Signing in as Mrs. Lottie A. Bernard, the woman attracted attention to herself from the start. She was traveling alone—frowned upon by Victorian society—and without luggage. She kept anxiously inquiring at the desk—not about her 'husband,' the missing Mr. Bernard, but a man she said was her 'brother.' Her brother, Dr. M.C. Anderson, was supposedly due at any time to help her with a vague but serious ailment. She never mentioned the husband. Both men would prove to be as fictional as Lottie A. Bernard herself. Both were part of the haunting mystery of Coronado that would endure for generations, and still today.

Over the next few days, she made odd requests of hotel staff (some of them downright chilling when reviewed in the light of new theories). Her health deteriorated rapidly, so that by Monday, November 28, four days after her arrival, she had difficulty walking. Nevertheless, she made an arduous journey—on foot, by trolley, and by ferry boat—to downtown San Diego, where she bought a gun and some ammunition. She returned to the hotel and was last seen on a balcony with other guests, staring westward at the impending arrival of a great sea storm. The next morning, an electrician found her dead on the back steps, a gunshot wound to her head, and that same gun lying by her side. The Deputy Coroner and his men took the body across the bay to San Diego, where she lay in state for at least two weeks. Thousands of Victorians—mostly women—came to view her embalmed and well-dressed body as if she were a dead princess or, more to the point, a fallen Victorian angel in the best sentimental traditions of the age. The story became an instant national sensation in the scandal-mongering Yellow Press. Daily telegraph dispatches crossed the wires with the latest breathless news, gossip, and innuendoes. What had she been up to? Why had she died? The mystery deepened as people started to realize she wasn't who she said she was. But who was she really?

Even as the police were looking for the illusory Dr. Anderson and a presumed Mr. Bernard, the corpse's identification shifted to that of Elizabeth 'Lizzie' Wyllie, a pregnant and troubled young beauty from Detroit.

That identification was clouded by the allegation that she was really a missing housemaid named Katie Logan from Los Angeles.

Briefly, she was thought to be a renter from Anaheim named Josie Brown. She was also thought to be the wife of a gambler named L. A. Bernard from Iowa.

Except Lizzie Wyllie, all of these women turned out to be fictions, and part of the pattern was that each had a mysterious doctor-brother orbiting unseen somewhere on the periphery, exerting some dark authoritative force that gave Kate Morgan's schemes some ephemeral credibility. Finally, the dead woman was reported to be Kate Morgan of Hamburg, Iowa, a shady lady of many false identities, unknown but dark secrets, and a pungent aura of sexual disgrace that electrified the Victorian imagination. The Kate Morgan legend persists to this day. Nobody has figured out why she came to the hotel, what really went on while she stayed there, or why she shot herself. Some even claim she was murdered.

I suggest in this book that the dead woman was not Kate Morgan but Lizzie Wyllie. If there is a ghost at the Hotel del Coronado, it is that of Lizzie Wyllie, who wants us to know it is she who is buried in a lonely grave up on Market Street, at that time outside town, in Mount Hope Cemetery. I think the mystery of why she appeared under a false name at this great resort was a blackmail plot gone horribly wrong. The owner of the hotel was the only man left standing financially after San Diego's terrible financial collapse of 1889—John Spreckels, heir to a fabulous Hawai'i sugar fortune, and one of the richest men in the United States. Kate Morgan was a ruthless schemer who dreamed up this blackmail scheme. She draped herself in false names with the same ease that Mata Hari tossed scarves about. Kate's target was Spreckels, the place of execution was his grand hotel, and her tool was a pregnant and desperate young Lizzie Wyllie. There were at least two men involved. One was John G. Longfield, Lizzie's lover and former book bindery foreman, a married man with several children, who had been fired from his job along with Lizzie and her sister May when word of their affair became known. The other was a shadowy figure, possibly Kate's husband Tom Morgan, or some lover of hers, who appeared briefly in a bank in Hamburg to help deliver a letter of credit for the alleged wife of 'a friend' in California—a woman named Lottie A. Bernard who was staying at the great hotel halfway across the country in Coronado.

I do not quite have a smoking gun, like a blackmail note. In fact, the woman at the Del was seen urgently burning a stack of papers in her hotel room, the day before she killed herself—and those probably included such documents. What convinces me of my case is how my theory solves every one of the dozens of loose ends that have dangled for over a century. It is an old and brittle case—a true cold case, in police parlance—that begins to make sense when you put all these many little pieces together in a way that every last detail makes sense. There are, in fact, several bits of evidence that are so egregious that it is almost laughable not to think that (a) the dead woman was Lizzie; (b) Kate Morgan was the planner who almost literally got away with murder; (c) Spreckels was the victim of a blackmail plot gone bad; and (d) there was a highly effective cover-up to protect John Spreckels. Those are highlights of the evidence I sort through in this book.

I believe I am the first to analyze the situation in its global context. The key to the analysis is John Spreckels. He owned the Hotel del Coronado. Though still based in San Francisco, he had bought or was buying up much of financially devastated greater San Diego, including Coronado. At the moment that Kate Morgan chose to strike with her ill-considered plan, John Spreckels was in Washington, D.C., lobbying with President Benjamin Harrison and Congress to prevent the overthrow of the Hawai'ian monarchy. The monarchy's fall would mean the loss of the Spreckels family's vast sugar plantations in the Hawai'ian kingdom, which the elder Claus Spreckels managed by controlling the monarchy and its royal cabinet appointments. Claus Spreckels was at that very same time doing desperate shuttle diplomacy between San Francisco and Honolulu. It is impossible to imagine that John Spreckels did not have an army of accountants, bankers, reporters, and other workers in San Diego to mind his affairs. That would include the local police and private security agents, possibly Pinkerton people. Spreckels owned the banks, the newspapers, all of Coronado, much of downtown San Diego, the light rail company, the utilities, the water flume, and anything else that could be bought and sold. Kate Morgan not only had an ill-conceived plan, but picked a bad time to put it into effect. As I will point out, there are moments when we can glimpse the dark hand of what I call the Spreckels Machine at work, shielding John Spreckels and his reputation at a time when his enemies would have been glad to smear him. As it would turn out, the corporate and missionary interests bent on ending Hawai'ian sovereignty—and getting it annexed as a U.S. territory—would win a huge victory less than a month after Lottie A. Bernard's death in Coronado. U.S. military and local militia deposed Queen Lili'uokalani at bayonet point on January 17, 1893, and a transitional government (followed by a short-lived republic ruled by Sanford Dole, cousin of the soon-to-be 'Pineapple King' James Dole) was established in preparation for annexation in 1897. On the hundredth anniversary of the annexation, in 1997, President Clinton and Congress would issue an official joint, bi-partisan apology to the Hawaiian people.

To fully understand what happened in the life and death of the 'Mysterious Stranger' at the Hotel del Coronado, it is necessary to understand both the local facts on the ground—outside the doors of the Hotel Del, and beyond what the official book covers—and the context, both national and global—in which those events took place.

And in the end, again, it comes down to the tragedy of Lizzie Wyllie—a beautiful woman, a fallen angel, a betrayed lover, and perhaps a grieving mother—who took her life when she saw no other recourse.

The Heritage Department's book is filled with more questions and mysteries than answers. My book picks up where the Heritage Department's book stops—at the border of speculation, where a weird scatter of myriad and ill-fitting facts lies like objects abandoned on the beach after a storm. With some daring, I thought my way through—from fact to puzzling fact, from mischievous clue to frustrating dead end, from loose end to logical trap—until I could finally make sense of it all. There was such a profusion of people's names and place names that I ended up drawing charts and maps, on which I connected people and places with variously colored pencil lines. When I published the first edition of my book in mid-2007, I decided to release it as historical fiction. After much deliberation and more insights—like about the sponge and medicine bottle that Lizzie ordered during her stay, of whose chilling implications I have more to say in this book—I am now confidently releasing this as nonfiction, true crime and history. It is the most comprehensive and coherent theory anyone has yet developed to explain a truly complex and tangled web of—yes—sex, violence, deceit, ruthless cunning, greed, and something approaching murder.

Some readers will find the ghost story more intriguing. Others will find that the ghost story pales in the shadow of an 1890s gaslamp true crime mystery that is contemporaneous with the world of Sherlock Holmes and Queen Victoria. Both realms will intrigue you.

There are actually two layers of conspiracy. The inner conspiracy (in which Kate Morgan was the driving force) stretch from Coronado to other cities around the U.S. We can begin organizing the endless profusion of named cities into several clusters of interest: Lake Ontario (Toronto, Cleveland, Detroit, Grand Rapids); Iowa/Nebraska (Hamburg, Iowa); San Francisco (San Francisco, Hanford, Visalia); Los Angeles (Los Angeles, Orange, Anaheim); and of course San Diego (San Diego and Coronado).

Independent but relevant is the global conspiracy in which the Spreckels family played their historic and losing defense. Those tentacles of conspiracy (framing the smaller conspiracy at the Hotel del Coronado) reached around the globe, from Honolulu to London, from San Francisco to Washington, D.C. They involved the last King and Queen of Hawai'i; a beautiful and tragic Crown Princess of Hawai'ian-Scottish origin; and indirectly the Empress of India herself, Queen Victoria, after whom Crown Princess Victoria Ka'iulani was named.

Part II. Ghost Story

Some Like It Spooky

Haunted Hotel

The Hotel del Coronado is a U.S. National Landmark, floating like a vast white fairy castle with brick-red turrets over a remarkable vista under clear blue skies. She sits on a long white beach overlooking the Pacific Ocean's placid expanse—framed to her west by palm-encrusted cliffs, and to the south by Mexican beaches. The view could be straight out of the South Sea Islands described by Robert Louis Stevenson in his pirate adventures (a topic not as far removed from the conversation of this book as you'd think—more on that in the Epilog, where we discuss another beautiful and tragic woman, young Crown Princess Victoria Ka'iulani).

The Hotel del Coronado is a great rambling sugar-white confection, whose design makes up in beauty what she omits in symmetry. She is one of the only surviving Victorian structures of her size and genre in the world. The grounds sprawl over about 31 acres of prime seascape property along the Pacific Ocean in the exclusive City of Coronado (pop. 26,600), which lies across the bay from the City of San Diego (metropolitan pop. 1.3 million). The original hotel contains over 330 rooms. The modern Ocean Towers and Cabanas add yet another 330 or more rooms, for a total of 679.[2] She holds over 1,000 guests when fully occupied, most of the year. At least one of those guests, it has long been rumored, is a ghost.

ಎ ⋘

Arguably, the most enduring guest and legend in the Hotel Del's history is its famous ghost.[3] There are at least two ghost stories associated with the Hotel Del, actually. The dead woman stayed in Room 302 (now 3327) overlooking Orange Avenue. As you approach the hotel, heading east on Orange Avenue coming from the Bay side, look toward the hotel approaching on your right at the intersection of Orange Avenue and R. H. Dana Place (which turns into Adella Avenue on the left side of Orange Avenue). Look straight from the street corner over the fence, at the square white tower with the miter-shaped dark red roof. From there, look down to the right at the curving corner of the building, which at that point is convex pointing toward you. You see two low roofs, atop thin white pillars, and the second floor windows behind those. On the next floor up, the third floor of four stories, is the triple set of windows through which Lottie A. Bernard gazed over Victorian Coronado.

The list of reported ghostly incidents surrounding that room, and other areas of the hotel, is legion. Some are documented at length in the Heritage Department's book. I will relate a few in this book. If the ghost is real, what would be the purpose of her haunting and her capricious activities? I believe it would be to try and communicate the truth about who she really was (Lizzie Wyllie, not Kate Morgan) and what really happened. One hears that ghosts live in the moment. Usually it is the moment of their sudden and often violent death. Perhaps, in that moment, she is still trying to reach out to her grieving mother, Elizabeth, and her sister, May, in Detroit. Everyone else in her life had betrayed her, especially her lover, John G. Longfield—and Kate Morgan, whom she had trusted, but who probably stole Longfield from her, and used her and the baby growing within her to commit a crime against John Spreckels. Lizzie was, to put it bluntly, a beautiful airhead without much common sense, but she never harmed anyone, and she clearly showed regret and remorse at involving herself in Kate Morgan's conspiracies. She was the only person in the saga with any genuine, admirable emotions. That makes her victimhood and cruel, lonely death all the more tragic. She really was that Victorian ideal of the Pre-Raphaelites and of Dickens' readership—the good angel, brought low by the machinations of evil people in a cruel and senseless world.

❧ ❦

Ghosts and ghost stories have been with us since the beginning of the human race. Many primitive peoples burned or crushed their dead out of fear that otherwise they might walk again at night. Ghost stories have been told around campfires since Paleolithic times, as some of the ancient cave paintings around the world suggest. Most cultures believe in the survival of the soul beyond death, and that not all souls wander off into some reward, but a few wayward ones get stuck for one reason or another and stay behind to frighten the living. Ancient Roman and Greek culture was rife with ghost stories. Among the Romans, it was more common for the ghost to be described as wearing a black toga while scaring the daylights out of people. In fact, the Romans were animists who believed in a profusion of spirits living in a parallel shamanistic world. They believed in countless *numina* (from *numen*, a nod or gesture) who inhabited every nook and cranny of the world. In the household, it was the ancestor spirits, or *lares*, and they had their altar in the entrance of the house. The father and sons of the household were the priests of the *lares*, and tended their shrine or *lararium*, which occupied a closet-like structure along with the death masks of the ancestors—and these ancestors haunted every house. The mother and daughters were priestesses of the kitchen part of the house, which was haunted by the *penates*, literally 'cupboard gods.' The custom was to throw a crust into the fire at each meal, and a few drops of wine on the floor, to appease them. These ancient customs are just a few that have survived into modern Italy in the form of *stregheria*, or witchcraft. Since Rome occupied most of Europe for centuries, something of the Roman culture survives in both northern and southern Europe as well as North Africa, the Middle East, and Britain. Every culture has its wealth of scary stories, and ours is no exception. One only needs to look at the popularity of books and films like William Blatty's 1973 story *The Exorcist* to realize the power of these ideas in modern society. What's remarkable about that movie is not only that people were badly affected while viewing it—a whole urban lore also sprang up about deaths among those who worked on the film, fire on the set, and so forth. Some of this lore parallels the 'Curse of the Pharaohs' legends that followed discovery of the XIII Dynasty Egyptian Pharaoh Tut-Ankh-Amun's tomb in 1922 by Howard Carter.

In contrast with all the black tales and nightmares since ancient and medieval times, including *succubi* that torment people in their sleep, and vampires who drink our blood, the ghost at the Hotel del Coronado is a very light touch. That doesn't mean she won't scare you out of your wits.

A friend of mine moved into management at the hotel, and a few weeks later I asked him if he was aware of any ghostly doings. He told me, with a bemused expression, that he had only a few days earlier received notice of a 'dead move' during the night. The expression 'dead move,' from which this book gets its name, is a hotel industry term for moving someone's belongings from one room to another. The case my friend referred to is one that often happens at the Del—in Room 3327 in particular (though 3519 is said to be heavily haunted also). The notoriety of Room 3519 is that a maid is said to have hung herself long ago in it. This maid is sometimes associated with the housekeeper mentioned in connection with Lottie A. Bernard, though the maid's name is unknown; the story is likely just urban lore.

The hotel's official policy is not to rent out Room 3327 unless it is the only room available and a guest specifically requests it. The story my friend related is fairly common. Often, a guest will light-heartedly and skeptically ask for Room 3327, and then become so frightened during the night that they call the front desk downstairs in a panic and demand to be moved immediately—a dead move, in the dead of night.

Part III. What We Know For Sure

Lottie A. Bernard Timeline

Day 0—Wednesday, Nov. 23, 1892 (Katie Logan in L.A.)

We'll call this Day Zero because it is the last day of one daring fraud, and the transition into another daring fraud that starts the next day.

Day Zero—the day before Thanksgiving, 1892—was last day of an imaginary person named Mrs. Katie Logan. Katie Logan worked for several weeks in Los Angeles, as a domestic servant for at least three wealthy families, the last of whom was the family of contractor L. A. Grant. This Katie Logan would, the following afternoon (Day 1), wink out of existence. She would transition into yet another fraudulent persona— Mrs. Lottie Anderson Bernard, baptized with the ink flowing from a desk clerk's dipping pen in the softly lit Hotel del Coronado lobby. Lottie A. Bernard was fated for a brief, five-day life whose termination resulted in the death of a real and unknown person.

The twenty-four hour period from sometime in the middle of Day Zero, when Katie Logan said goodbye to the L. A. Grant family in Los Angeles, to the signing-in of Lottie A. Bernard at the Hotel del Coronado during the next afternoon, is also known as 'The Missing Day.' The Missing Day addresses the question of why the two-hour train trip from Los Angeles took her a whole day. Does it matter? What if she just went shopping, or goofed off? But she didn't. As we will see, she was heading south on a train from Los Angeles to San Diego, at the same time that a witness placed her on a train from Denver headed to Orange (halfway between Los Angeles and San Diego). On that train, she had a heart-wrenching argument with a cruel-seeming man—possibly her lover. So the Missing Day will be very interesting for us to figure out. It is one of several mysteries within a mystery that has long festered in the soul of the Lottie Bernard saga. When I present my theory in the next section, I will propose an answer for this, and all other questions in this complex saga. Even the names Lottie and Charlotte have special significance.

Bear in mind, none of what happened on Day Zero became known until well after Lottie Bernard's death. On the day of the Coroner's Inquest, November 30, 1892, six days after she signed in at the Hotel Del, it was assumed she really was Mrs. Lottie Anderson Bernard. As far as the nine men on the Coroner's jury were concerned, she appeared out of nowhere on November 24, our Day One.

From Day Zero, we now follow the known facts in chronological sequence. Katie Logan was well-liked by the L. A. Grants, and they fully expected her to return the next day to help with Thanksgiving dinner. She would never be seen again. Stored at the L. A. Grants' home was a trunk that would be opened many days later by Los Angeles police—revealing startling clues that nobody has really examined in context until now. The solution to the Lottie Bernard mystery (or Kate Morgan mystery) begins taking shape at the L. A. Grants' house—in that trunk, which we'll examine in greater detail soon.

Day 1—Thursday, Nov. 24, 1892 (Lottie Bernard Checks In)

An attractive young woman stepped from the train sometime in the late morning hours of Thanksgiving Day. She was traveling alone—a fact frowned upon in Victorian times—with only a hand satchel and the clothes on her back.

The original San Diego train station was built 1887 during the same economic boom that saw the Hotel del Coronado constructed. The station was an ornate, one-story wooden Victorian structure[4] with a short but imposing clock tower. It was demolished in 1915, and replaced by today's Union Station or Santa Fe Depot.

She went to the baggage office near the old train station and spoke with a clerk at a window. She told him she needed to check out her three trunks. The clerk asked her for the baggage claim checks ('checks') or tickets. She told him her 'brother'[5] had them, and she had gotten separated from him. This is the 'brother' of whom we shall hear time and again. The clerk refused to turn over the luggage, and the woman left with only her hand satchel.

She did not immediately head to the ferry landing to cross over to Coronado. Instead, witnesses would later state that she walked some ten blocks east on C Street to the Hotel Brewster.[6] The Hotel Brewster was a large new hotel on the corner of 4th and C Streets. Created during the 1880s boom years, it was designed to be efficient, clean, and safe for traveling businessmen. The purpose of the woman's detour has remained unknown until now, but I will offer an explanation. Witnesses claimed she asked about her brother (the sometime 'doctor') and his wife. Hotel staff told her they were not known at the Brewster.

From the Hotel Brewster, she walked or rode to the Coronado ferry landing on the San Diego side. Today's ferry landing is at the foot of West Broadway (then D Street) in San Diego. At that time, the ferry landing was near the foot of H Street (today's Market Street, on the waterfront near what is today the area around Tuna Lane by the Aircraft Carrier Midway Museum).

That's approximately one mile as the crow flies, or a walk equivalent to about fifteen city blocks. She might have walked through the Stingaree, one of the most notorious red light districts on the West Coast. More likely, she traveled back down C Street to the rail depot, and then turned left to walk south along the harbor shore some five or six blocks to the ferry landing. She was known to be in robust health at this time, and the walk would hardly have strained her.

It is possible, but not very likely, that she could have traveled to Coronado on the Belt Line,[7] which circled the Bay from San Diego to Coronado, via National City and what are today Chula Vista and Imperial Beach. The ferry ride was the shortest way to cross the Bay, and one is inclined to think she used this route. She boarded one of the large metal ferries then operating, collectively known as the 'Nickel Snatcher' because the fare was five cents. These vessels were large enough to carry horses and buggies—unlike today's ferry, which is moderate in size, and can accommodate bicycles. She may well have ridden on the side-wheeler *Coronado*, 208 tons and built of steel, commissioned 1886. Another ferry boat in service was the large steamer *Ramona*.[8]

The crossing was about a quarter mile. She disembarked some fifteen minutes later at the Coronado ferry terminal, a few hundred feet north (at today's Centennial Park) of today's Ferry Landing Marketplace in the City of Coronado. Bits of the old concrete wharf are still visible along the Centennial Park shoreline.

Coronado (incorporated as a city in 1891) sits on a portion of the Peninsula of San Diego.[9] As with much of the background detail given here, it is helpful information in understanding the Lottie Bernard saga.

From the ferry landing, she walked three or four minutes to First and Orange, where she boarded the little Coronado trolley for the 1.3 mile ride to the Hotel del Coronado.

☙ ❧

So it came to be that the 'Beautiful Stranger' checked into the lobby of the Hotel del Coronado, using the name Lottie A. Bernard. It was early to mid-afternoon on Thanksgiving Day, Thursday, November 24, 1892.[10] She immediately attracted attention, not only because of her charm and beauty, but because she was traveling alone and without any luggage except her small handbag. Clerks thought her 'peculiar.'[11] Victorians felt it reflected badly on a woman's moral character to travel alone, without her husband, a male family member, or an older female chaperone.

HOTEL DEL CORONADO,		
E. S. BABCOCK, Manager.		Coronado, California.
Money, Jewels, and other valuable Packages, must be placed in the Safe in the office, otherwise the Proprietor will not be responsible for any loss.		
NAMES.	RESIDENCE.	ROOMS.
Thursday Nov. 24th 1892		
Mark J. Williams	N.Y. City	300
Frary Perrin	Pawtucket R.I.	15
Mrs R. H. Gage	Pawtucket R.I.	153
Mrs M.E. French	Pawtucket R.I.	153
Geo Nest	Detroit N.Y.	113
Mrs R. Irwin	Denver Colo	315
Grace Irwin	Denver Colo	315
Miss Lottie A Bernard	Detroit	302
Jack Jones	Boston	371
Ira Clark + wife	Coronado	
Fran & Clark	"	
H.C. Moon	Newmex	196

She stepped up to the dark wood counter (at a special side window reserved for women) and asked the clerk to sign her in. Most people signed the guest register themselves, but it was not unheard-of for a clerk to provide that courtesy. She gave her name as Mrs. Lottie A. Bernard of Detroit, Michigan.

A few things are notable about the guest register, whose page has come down to us as a historical artifact.[12] It appears that twelve persons signed in that day (there is a termination line at the bottom of the page, and there are various check marks that suggest the page was proofed by the chief clerk or an auditor, as a matter of daily routine). A nicely rounded dot above the scrawled word 'Mrs.' on her line suggests that she may have first said "Miss" and then changed it to 'Mrs.' In fact, a close examination suggests the confused clerk perhaps wrote 'Mis.' In the upper left hand corner, the name 'E. S. Babcock, Manager' is given. That was Elisha Babcock, who conceived and executed a breathtaking plan to develop a magnificent resort across the bay from San Diego, on a section of the barren Peninsula of San Diego known as South Island (also known as Coronado Island, no relationship to the Coronado Islands some miles off shore that are owned by the municipality of Tijuana, Mexico).

Together with his friend, Chicago piano fortune heir Hampton Story, and Jacob Gruendike, president of the First National Bank of San Diego, Babcock founded the Coronado Beach Company and developed what would soon become the City of Coronado. With the proceeds from the land sales, Babcock built the sprawling sugar-baker palace of white walls and brick-red turrets called the Hotel del Coronado in 1887. It opened February 1888 to receive its first guest.

In the meantime, San Francisco sugar fortune heir John Spreckels (1853-1926), who had discovered the beauty and mild climate of San Diego during an 1887 yacht visit, bought out Story and Gruendike's interests in the Coronado Beach Company, and thus became co-owner of the Del with Elisha Babcock. In 1889, the worst economic collapse in San Diego history caused the population to plummet from (an estimated) 44,000 to about 16,000 people—roughly the population before the boom. During the economic downturn, Babcock had to borrow money to keep the operation afloat, and he turned to John Spreckels.

John Spreckels was one of the sons of a remarkable, self-made man named Claus Spreckels (1828-1908), a German immigrant who arrived penniless in the U.S. in the 1840s and built several fortunes involving groceries. Claus Spreckels had several sons, of whom oldest son John appears to have been his right-hand man. Claus Spreckels became known as the Sugar Baron, because he owned huge cane sugar plantations in Hawai'i, and, along with a small group of cronies, virtually controlled the islands' economy and much of the Pacific sugar trade. He also shaped the Hawai'ian political landscape by controlling appointments to the king's cabinet. This was bitterly resented by a group of primarily conservative U.S. Protestant missionaries who had tried to ban Hawai'ian traditions they found offensive, like hula dancing, singing, and scant clothing. The missionary faction was allied with a coterie of armed Whites known as the Honolulu Rifles, and with U.S. corporations led by a cousin (James Ballard Dole) of the soon to be 'Pineapple King,' Sanford Dole. Together, they formed a secret society called the Hawai'ian League, which strongly militated toward Hawai'i's annexation by the United States. This faction held a near-coup in 1887, imposing the so-called Bayonet Constitution. They removed most of the king's powers, and took voting and property rights from nearly all Asians in favor of wealthy U.S. and European whites. After the overthrow of the monarchy (January 17, 1893, just seven weeks after Lottie A. Bernard's death), James Dole was on his way to become president of a republic.

By the time Lottie Bernard checked in at the Hotel del Coronado, the balance of powers in Hawai'i had become very shaky. At that very moment, John Spreckels, owner of the Hotel del Coronado, was in Washington lobbying President Benjamin Harrison and the Congress to prevent a takeover of Hawai'i. At the same time, the elder Claus Spreckels was en route to Honolulu for desperate, last-minute shuttle diplomacy to try and save the dynasty of Queen Lili'uokalani. By this time, John Spreckels' financial holdings in San Diego were already vast. He owned most of Coronado, much of downtown San Diego, the local newspaper, the utilities, the light rails, the telegraph, and just about anything else. When Elisha Babcock was deep in debt, John Spreckels called his loans. Babcock was unable to produce payment, so Spreckels offered him a deal in lieu of foreclosure. Spreckels became the sole owner of the Hotel. He forgave Babcock's debts, paid him a large sum of money, and kept him on as General Manager. Hence, the heading at top left in the guest register, which identified Babcock as General Manager.

I believe here lies the key to the entire mystery: John Spreckels was the target of Kate Morgan's blackmail plot, using a gullible, naïve, and very attractive young girl from Detroit—Lizzie Wyllie, pregnant, in love, in trouble, and increasingly desperate as she began to realize she was being betrayed by the very two persons she needed and trusted most: Kate Morgan, and Lizzie's lover John G. Longfield.

Lottie appears to have paid on a day by day basis, the only one checking in that day who did. This is judging by the notation in the rightmost column of the guest register,[13] where a "D" is written on her line. The other guests are either indicated by an "S" (presumably short term, or weekly) or an "L" (long term, or monthly). Lottie took Room 302, on the third floor, a reasonably spacious room (about 12 by 15 feet) with three windows in an angled or curved configuration, overlooking the intersection of Orange Avenue (Coronado's main street) and Richard Henry Dana Place. From that intersection, a half a block south along Dana Place takes you to the beach and Ocean Boulevard.

If one stands in that room today (now Room 3327), one looks kitty-corner across a parking lot toward the intersection, with Orange Avenue on the right, and R. H. Dana Place coming into view on the left as an extension of Ocean Boulevard (not visible). In other words, the room faces away from the sea. As one drives along the Pacific shore on Ocean Boulevard, the boulevard turns into R. H. Dana Place along the western side of the hotel, crosses Orange Avenue, and turns into tiny Adella Avenue. This is today probably Coronado's busiest pedestrian intersection, with heavy foot traffic coming from the beach and the Hotel del Coronado, and many little shops along either side of Orange Avenue.

During Lottie Bernard's day, the Coronado Beach Rail Road trolley line ran between the Hotel Del and the Ferry Landing, and Lottie took that trolley several times, including on her final, deadly errand to buy the gun that killed her. The trolley was at that time a two-car affair, the one being a little steam engine (or 'steam dummy') disguised as a trolley car to avoid scaring horses, and the driver sat in there; the other car was a light rail platform with four completely open bays, each containing two wooden seats capable of holding about three persons, so that the trailer could probably hold two dozen people when full. Orange Avenue is so called because, when the trolley was eliminated, a long stand of orange trees was planted where the tracks had been. The oranges, however, were a favorite food of the jack rabbits that still infested the peninsula, so the orange trees were removed in favor of a manicured grassy strip running the entire 1.3 mile distance of Orange Avenue from the Hotel Del on the Pacific coast side (south, because the beach there runs east-west). Orange Avenue briefly runs west, then curves northeastward through Spreckels Park in the center of Coronado, to Centennial Park and the Ferry Landing and Market Place overlooking the beautiful San Diego skyline on the Bay side in a northeasterly direction.

Looking out from Lottie's room toward the intersection of Dana/Orange/Adella, one sees a low, Spanish-style building (now the Hotel El Cordoba and various shops and restaurants, built in 1902 as a mansion for Elisha Babcock). Moving one's eyes toward the right along Orange Avenue, one sees several hotels, including the upscale Glorietta Bay Inn, named after the street and the bay east of there. This white mansion was constructed after the 1906 San Francisco earthquake disaster, when John Spreckels permanently moved his family to San Diego and ensconced them in this palatial estate overlooking Glorietta Bay (now housing the Coronado Yacht Club) on the east, and Spreckels' grand hotel across the street looking south.

When Lottie took up residence in Room 302, third floor rooms were traditionally cheapest. The best rooms were on the ground floor, in this age before widespread elevators, because wealthy guests did not expect to walk up and down flights of stairs. The Hotel actually has one of the oldest functioning elevators anywhere—Otis Number 61, dating from at or around the Hotel's opening in 1888. Each room had its own little fireplace, with a vent to the roof. During renovations over the years, the fireplaces were removed and replaced with central heating. When the Cabanas and Ocean Towers were constructed in the late 20th Century, men digging along the beach property east of the original hotel uncovered a mass of brick wreckage where the old fireplaces had been buried. Today's Room 3327 has a full bath where the fireplace was at one time. In her day, Lottie used a communal bathroom (and tub for bathing) down the hall.

Lottie befriended a bellman (or 'bellboy') named Harry West on her first evening.[14] She told Harry she suffered from neuralgia—not today's more specific neurological disorder by the same name, but a vague nervous ailment commonly diagnosed in that era, covering all sorts of psychological and neurological disorders (and no small amount of hypochondria). She also told Harry that she was waiting for her 'brother,' who by now had acquired a name—Dr. M. C. Anderson of Indianapolis. This is now the second 'man' in her life. She would want us to assume the first 'man' was a putative 'husband' (since she signed in as Mrs. Lottie A. Bernard)—the presumed Mr. Bernard, for whom police across the country searched vainly after her death. Like Lottie herself, both of the men were fictions.

She was vigorous and healthy when she checked in. A young fellow employed by Star Stables, Charlie Stevens, took her on a long ride around town,[15] and he later told people that she seemed in good health, though he implied she seemed a bit preoccupied or sad.

Day 2—Friday, Nov. 25, 1892

Early in the day, she spoke with Chief Clerk A. S. Gomer. She explained that her luggage was locked up in the baggage depot near the train station in downtown San Diego. This was the same story she told others at the hotel, and which was repeated in the Coroner's Inquest—and mutated after her death into quite a different story by the apocryphal testimony of a train traveler from Denver, Joseph A. or Joseph E. Jones of Boston. Jones' comments to a bellman throw light on the notorious 'Missing Day' of this saga, as we shall see. Lottie A. Bernard told Gomer that she had been traveling with her brother, but that they became separated on the trains at Orange, California (about an hour north, near today's Disneyland at Anaheim, and roughly halfway between San Diego and Los Angeles). She said that her brother had the tickets in his pocket, that she didn't know where her brother was, and that the baggage clerks would not release her trunks without the tickets. According to Gomer (at the Coroner's Inquest) she asked daily, with growing anxiety, if word had come from her 'brother' (neither Kate Morgan nor Lizzie Wyllie is known to have had a brother, but Kate Morgan often used the 'brother' and 'doctor' ruse during what can only have been scams).

Day 3—Saturday, Nov. 26, 1892

On the third day at the Hotel del Coronado, real estate agent T. J. Fisher testifies she came into the hotel drugstore, where he shared an office with the druggist. Fisher says she wandered about 'slowly' and apparently 'in pain.' She asked for medicine to ease her pain (described as 'intense suffering'). Fosdick suggested she consult a doctor, and she brushed this aside, telling him that her brother, a physician, would be arriving any day to care for her—the elusive 'Dr. Anderson,' who would never show up nor send word.

Later in the day, Harry West rather vaguely remembered that she asked him to get her an empty pint bottle and a sponge from the hotel drugstore. No reason is known why she wanted these items, but, like so many tiny details, they are significant, and downright chilling, in my theory—as I will explain in the next section, *Part IV: Solved!*.

Day 4—Sunday, Nov. 27, 1892

No activity known.

Day 5—Monday, Nov. 28, 1892

During the morning on the fifth day, Lottie had Harry West bring her a glass of wine from the bar, and later a whiskey cocktail. Harry prepared a bath for her (down the hall from her room), and brought her a pitcher of ice water she requested. She told him she would be in the bath for an hour or two.

Around noon, Lottie returned to her room and rang for Harry West. He would later testify that he found her suffering and groaning a great deal, and sleeping much of the day. She told him she had fallen in the tub and gotten her hair wet, and she asked him to dry it for her. It appears that she fell because she was weak, that she felt her wet hair would worsen her illness, and that she was too weak to dry it. Harry toweled her hair dry. He would later tell investigators that she seemed to sleep a while, wake up, spend time groaning in pain, and then fall back to sleep. He said she again mentioned that Dr. Anderson, who would soon join her.

Between noon and 1:00 p.m., Harry told Gomer, his superior, that he had brought Lottie a whiskey. Gomer testified that he had suggested, through a female housekeeper, that Lottie have a doctor see her.

Gomer went to the room to inquire about her health, and also about her finances. Apparently she was paying her room charge daily, but she was running up an expense tab on the side, which a guest would customarily pay when checking out. Gomer was keeping a worried eye on this tab.

It was a cold, dreary, gloomy day—a huge sea storm was approaching, which would lash the region fiercely all night, and then subside by morning. Barometric pressure was falling, and there was a growing air of dreadful anticipation as the violent storm approached. This storm would set the mood for events that followed. Gomer found her as Harry had described her—sick, in bed, suffering. Gomer suggested she light a fire in her fireplace, but she refused. She then told him a story that she was near death from stomach cancer (which Dr. Mertzman would later deride as virtually impossible). Whereas before she had said Dr. Anderson would take care of her when he arrived, now she said the doctors had given up on her and death was just around the corner. It sounds as though she was simply trying to get rid of Gomer, who appears to have been a somewhat fussy and inquisitive man, concerned about guests and goings-on at the hotel where he held some responsibility.

Gomer—no doubt because of her 'peculiarity' and alarming condition—was concerned whether she would be able to pay her tab. Lottie urged Gomer to telegraph a Mr. G. L. Allen in Hamburg, Iowa, who would wire the needed funds.

During the afternoon, Lottie rang for some matches. Harry West offered to bring a whole box, but she said she only needed a few matches (he had some in his pocket, which he gave her) to burn a stack of papers (possibly including letters) in the fireplace. Neither Gomer nor Harry got a good look at what these papers might be. From notes she wrote, which the coroner found in her room, it seems she had much on her mind.

That afternoon, Lottie went downstairs to the pharmacy. Real estate agent T. J. Fisher described her as walking very slowly, and appearing to be in great pain. During their conversation, she indicated she planned to go across the Bay to San Diego, and he warned her against doing so—because of her condition and the coming storm. Lottie replied that she had to go, and then made a statement that appears somewhat unfocused and out of kilter with already established facts (or fibs).[16] From what Fisher quoted at the Coroner's Inquest, she said that she must make the trip. She said that she forgot her baggage 'checks' [claim tickets], and that she must go across the Bay "to identify my trunks, personally."

Between 4:00 and 5:00 p.m. (there is confusion about whether she was in San Diego as early as 3:00 p.m., or later) Lottie journeyed to downtown San Diego. She rode the little Coronado Beach R.R. trolley mentioned earlier, with its steam dummy and trailer, to the ferry landing. Witnesses said she appeared so weak that, as she left the Hotel del Coronado, she had to be helped onto the little streetcar by the conductor.

She took the ferry across the bay, a 15 minute ride to cross a quarter mile of water. She stepped ashore near G Street in the City of San Diego, and walked several blocks to Fifth Avenue (in the heart of today's Gaslamp Quarter). She probably skirted the violent, noisy Stingaree district at the southern end of Fifth Street (today's Fifth Avenue near the baseball stadium).

She walked into a store called the Ship Chandlery at 624 Fifth Street,[17] and asked clerk Frank Heath if he sold revolver cartridges. He testified she seemed 'nervous or excited.' She spoke in a very low (or soft) voice and appeared to be sick. She walked slowly and looked 'very bad.' Heath, who noted she was very well dressed, told her he did not sell cartridges, and directed her to Chick's Gun Shop at 1663 Sixth Street.

M. Chick testified that Lottie walked into the store and asked if he had a gun she could buy for a friend as a Christmas present. He sold her a revolver and cartridges, and showed her how to load and fire the weapon. A witness, W. P. Walters, observed this, and remarked to another bystander that that woman was going to "hurt herself with that pistol."

Lottie left Chick's Gun Shop and walked south on Fifth Street toward the store of Schiller & Murtha's at Fifth Street and D Avenue.[18] Her movements from there are unknowns, but the general direction seems to have been toward the ferry landing.

At 6:30 p.m., says bellman Harry West at the inquest, he saw Lottie on a hotel veranda overlooking the ocean. It was dark by then, and an air of dread and excitement hung in the air as the atmospheric monster approached. It was the last time Harry would see Lottie alive.

Lottie made one more stop at the front desk to ask Gomer if there was any word from Dr. Anderson. That was between 7:00 and 8:00 p.m., and Gomer said there was not yet any word from her 'brother.' This was the last time anyone saw her alive.

People stood on balconies all around the Hotel, looking south and west over the Pacific Ocean. They watched in awe as the black clouds of the storm rolled closer, and raged and thundered. It is likely that some guests may have requested relocation to the landward side of the Hotel, because nobody heard a gunshot fired during the night, on the beach just behind the hotel.

Day 6—Tuesday, Nov. 29, 1892 (Body Found)

Electrician David Cone discovered her body at 8:20 a.m. Cone was walking his daily rounds, 'trimming the lights,' which probably meant manually turning off some (especially outdoor) lights.

అ ఈ

As is typical of the San Diego region, the storm vented its fury during the night, and quickly passed, leaving a mild and foggy silence. By daylight, the storm was long gone. The electrician David Cone came across the grotesque scene of a mannequin-like body lying on the concrete steps overlooking the beach, which was not far from the sea in those days. When he realized it was a woman's dead body, he saw that her clothing was all wet, and the body "seemed to have been lying there quite a while, to have been dead quite a while."[19]

The body lay in something like a sitting position on the concrete steps, with its feet toward the ocean. There was a gun by its side, and blood on the steps. A 'large pistol' lay to her right. Her clothes were soaked. Cone was utterly shaken, and hurried to report the find to his superiors. Along the way, he encountered a gardener named F. W. Koeppen, with whom he returned to the crime scene. The two men separated and ran in opposite directions around the Hotel. Koeppen ran to inform the assistant manager, Mr. Rossier, while Cone ran to tell the chief clerk. Cone eventually went back to his duties of 'trimming' the lights. Koeppen brought Rossier to the steps, where the two men covered the body with a tarp. Koeppen stayed with the corpse until the coroner's men arrived.

That morning, when chief clerk A.S. Gomer opened his office, he received a telegram from a Hamburg, Iowa bank, in which $25 credit was extended to one Lottie A. Bernard. This was the credit she had promised, though it is not clear whether it satisfied her debt. US$25 in 1892 would be worth over $500 in early 21st Century U.S. dollars.[20] Compared to a laborer's estimated $1 a day at the time (hence 'another day, another dollar'), that should cover any services billed to her room, since there is no indication she did anything extravagant—she did tip Harry West a dollar for a trivial service at one point. Gomer wired back that the woman had died, and instructed the bank to contact the San Diego Coroner's office.

Between 9:30 and 10:00 a.m., Deputy Coroner H. J. Stetson arrived from the mainland with a crew to remove the body. Stetson estimated Lottie had been dead about six or seven hours, meaning she shot herself (or was murdered, by some urban lore) between 2:00 and 3:00 a.m. That would mean the body lay on the steps for up to seven hours as the storm abated. From the time of discovery to the time Stetson and his crew arrived, two hours passed—a remarkable short time. There was rudimentary telephone service to the mainland from the hotel itself, and there was always the telegraph. Stetson would then gather his men, walk or ride several blocks from the police headquarters on Fifth Street to the waterfront, and then ride the ferry ('the next boat'[21]) across to Coronado. The crossing took 15 minutes on the steam-powered ferry. Stetson and his men would then cross the island—1.3 miles to the Hotel del Coronado from the ferry landing— which can be walked in a leisurely twenty to thirty minutes. Stetson's crew took the body to Johnson & Company Mortuary, 907 Sixth Street. The same day, Stetson searched Lottie's room. He found several items of puzzling and tantalizing interest, which he was to describe at the Coroner's Inquest.

Day 7—Wednesday, Nov. 30, 1892 (Coroner's Inquest)

Newspaper Accounts

The Daily Bee (San Diego) reports[22] dramatically that Mrs. Lottie A. Bernard died at the Hotel del Coronado "...last night alone and desperate...on the stone stairs at the west end of the ocean terrace leading to the beach...the surf wrapped and then re-wrapped her with its spray, and the pitiless rain fell upon her bared head and young white face."

౭ ౼

The San Diego Union, Wednesday, November 30, the day of the coroner's inquest, gushingly and excitedly reports the finding of a body at the Hotel del Coronado the previous day at 8:20 a.m. by the electrician David Cone.

Hotel staff, who saw her when she was alive, described the woman as "attractive, prepossessing, and highly educated..."[23]

She wore black the night she died, with a lace shawl over her head when Harry West last saw her on a seaward veranda late Monday (between 9:00 and 10:00 p.m. Monday, Nov. 28).

The article describes a lashing "tempest that is sweeping over the whole coast" and says she ventured "within fifteen feet of the ocean's edge."[24]

Her body was cold and stiff. According to the article in the paper, the storm obliterated any blood stains.[25]

She checked in Thursday, Nov. 24, carrying only a small handbag.[26]

She was "frequently attended by a housekeeper," but this person was not called to testify at the inquest.

By November 28, she was so weak that she fell in the bath and had to have bellman Harry West dry her hair in her room. She is described as "nervous and unstrung." There are references to her being 'lonely' because she continually asked about her 'brother,' who never did show up (no doubt another alias for John Longfield.)

The article mentions that she had over $20 cash in her purse, or well over $240 in today's dollars (assuming a differential of 12 to 1 between 1892 vs. 2008 U.S. Dollars).

According to the article, telegrams about Lottie's death were sent to a bank officer in Hamburg, Iowa (who had extended $25 credit on Lottie's behalf to the Hotel del Coronado, as reported by chief clerk Gomer) and possible Bernard family members in Detroit (the city listed as Lottie's home at registration). In other words, it is clear at this point that the deceased is believed to truly be one Lottie A. Bernard.

The Coroner's Inquest

Shortly before the Coroner's Inquest was gaveled into session, the leading physician and surgeon in town, Dr. B. F. Mertzman, did a half-hour examination of the body. He was not permitted to autopsy her. He would testify at the inquest.

On November 30, the day after her death, per order of Deputy San Diego Coroner H. J. Stetson, a nine man jury gathers for a formal inquest. Justice of the Peace and Acting Coroner W. A. Sloane, Esq., gavels the session to order and calls witnesses to the stand.

David Cone, the electrician who first spotted the body, testifies that, around seven the previous morning, he was trimming the lights around the hotel after the great storm, when he came upon the dead woman's body. He testifies that she lay face up, near the top of the stairs and facing the ocean. He saw blood on the steps to the right of the body, and the body appeared to have lain there for some time. A 'large pistol' lay on the right beside the body.

Next, Sloane interrogates gardener F. W. Koeppen, who fetched the assistant manager, Rossier. They covered the body with a tarpaulin. The pistol lay untouched under the tarpaulin.

Next, Frank Heath of the Ship's Chandlery, 624 Fifth Street, testifies. He saw the dead woman in the store, and she asked for cartridges. She spoke in a low voice, nervously, and he had trouble understanding her. She was well dressed, and walked slowly and looked bad, as if she were sick.

Next, Dr. B. F. Mertzman, physician and surgeon, testifies. He was called in this morning, a half hour before the inquest (more than a day after David Cone's discovery of he body), to examine the corpse at Johnson & Company. He was not permitted to autopsy her. He has found an entry wound in the right temple, and no exit wound. The bullet traveled a little bit forward and a little bit upward. Mertzman estimates the caliber to be 'about .38 or .40.' There was no exit wound. The bullet stayed in the brain, despite the considerable caliber of the cartridge.

Next, real estate agent J. Fisher testifies. His existence at the Hotel Del is a direct, but anachronistic, result of the real estate boom of the late 1880s buoyed by Elisha Babcock's auctioneering of lots in Coronado before building the Del. Fisher testifies that he first saw the woman the previous Saturday, when she appeared to be suffering as she paced up and down in the arcade. Fisher says he sent her to Fosdick, the pharmacist. She ventured in again on Monday, and Fosdick advised her not to travel on account of her neuralgia and the coming storm, but she said she must look after her missing luggage.

Next, Harry West is asked to testify. He lives with his parents at 2519 I Street between 16th and 17th Streets. He says he saw her often. The last time he saw her was at half past six on Monday evening. She appeared to be in great pain, slept a great deal, and would wake up groaning.

Next, A. S. Gomer testifies. He says he can only identify her by the name she gave—Mrs. Lottie A. Bernard (or Barnard), Detroit. He says she arrived by way of Orange, and apparently lost her brother along the way—Dr. M. C. Anderson. Gomer noticed letters or documents in her room, that she intended to burn in the fireplace [but in no hurry, since she didn't want them to light a fire]. Says he saw two or three letters addressed by her, to herself, at a Detroit address. Says that a telegram arrived from Hamburg, IA, covering $25 funds.

Next, M. Chick, the gun shop owner, testifies. The woman wanted a gun for a Christmas present. She purchased a .44 American Bulldog. He looks at the pistol as the coroner holds it, and states that he cannot positively testify if that is the gun he sold the dead woman, but he seems to recognize a bit of rust on it. He describes how he showed her to load and fire it.

Next, W.P. Walters testifies. He had been a customer at Chick's Gun Shop. He saw the woman walk in very slowly, 'straight out' as if stiffly, and speak with Chick. She asked Chick to verify that the gun would be easy to operate. Chick showed her that the "pull" (on the trigger) was easy, and showed her how to load it. She had him put it in a box and wrapped. As she left, Walters heard another man say that the woman was 'going to hurt herself with that pistol.' Walters and another man followed her to the door, and determined that she went into at least two other retail establishments—Schiller & Murtha's, and The Combination.

Next, Deputy Coroner H. J. Stetson testifies that he was summoned (by telephone) to the hotel on the peninsula. He arrived to find the woman's body lying on the steps, covered by a tarpaulin. The undertakers followed on the next ferry, put it in a receiving box (a temporary coffin), and removed it to Johnson & Company in the city. He says that she was stiff and cold after lying there perhaps six or seven hours. He testifies that "the pistol was lying on the next step, the stone steps that go down to the surf, and her hand rested on the lower edge of one, and it had fallen out on to the edge of the next one below, and there was blood around it and underneath it."

Stetson further testifies that, while examining her room, he found a valise. He also found an envelope she had addressed to *Denman Thompson, The Old Homestead*. This refers to one of the most famous actors of the day, Denman Thompson of New Hampshire. According to a contemporary critic, "Thompson interpreted America to itself in the core persona of the solid New England farmer."

Stetson also found a piece of paper on which was written the word Frank four times: *Frank Frank Frank Frank*.

Stetson found another scrap of paper on which she had written: "I merely heard of that man. I do not know him." As with the rest of the artifacts in her room, we have no guess at an explanation, but we can imagine they elicited stunned silence and wonderment in the courtroom.

Stetson found an invitation, by Louise Leslie Carter and Lillian Russell, for Lottie to join them at the Hotel del Coronado. Carter and Russell were two of the most famous stage actresses of the day.

Stetson mentions another innocent little detail about yet another piece of critical evidence. In the room were several embroidered hankies. Some of them clearly had the name Louisa Anderson embroidered on them. Stetson stumbles over the name on some evidently more faded hankies, where the last name is clearly Anderson, but he says he can't read the first name— which he says looks like 'Little.'

Under further questioning, Stetson says that he examined the grate in the room, and found some papers that had burned entirely to ashes. A nightgown hung on a hook. On the mantel were a hat, a bottle, and a penknife. Among the other bottles in the room were one with camphor (a topical anesthetic) and alcohol—a considerable quantity of brandy. There were some quinine pills, and a bottle of some kind that had a notice wrapped around it: "If it does not relieve you, you better send for the doctor." The notice was signed "Druggist," without address.

Stetson testifies that when he came to the hotel, clerk A. S. Gomer informed him that a telegram had been received just that morning from a bank in Iowa, confirming that Mrs. Bernard's expense account would be honored to the amount of $25.00. Stetson asked Gomer to inform the bank of Mrs. Bernard's suicide, which Gomer did, but there has been no reply—in itself not surprising, since it has only been one day.

Stetson has not gone to inquire at the baggage office, but says he didn't bother "because she had no checks or anything put away, to know." Stetson says he knows nothing of her brother.

The coroner states that the court has received all the testimony it can get, and asks the jury to issue its finding. It is afternoon, and the entire proceeding has taken less than one day.

Newspaper Accounts Dec. 1-Dec. 14

Day 8—Thursday, Dec. 1, 1892

The San Diego Union reports that Kate traveled into San Diego just after noon Monday, Nov. 28, to buy a handgun.[27]

It is now established she traveled on the streetcar in Coronado, and both ways was with the same conductor (who, like so many other potential witnesses, was not called to testify at the inquest). According to the article, she went straight to buy a gun, and then returned immediately to Coronado.[28]

While riding on the trolley, she apparently asked for a hardware store (she most likely did not ask about a gun shop, which would have attracted more attention) and was referred to Todd & Hawley's hardware store.

At 6:30 p.m., Lottie once more checked with hotel staff[29] to see if they had received any letters or telegrams for her, or if her brother had come.

The article reports that handkerchiefs were found in her room, after her death, with the name 'Lottie Anderson' embroidered on them. They were said to be "of the finest linen."[30]

The article suggests that people are starting to wonder if there was more to the relationship between Lottie Bernard and her purported 'brother' than she had let on. If he was truly her brother, the reasoning went, he would have contacted authorities already, because news of her suicide had been telegraphed all over the country, and was being avidly followed by the Yellow Press. Already, there is speculation that the mysterious 'brother' was actually her lover. So quickly, the story in the Yellow Press took on a salacious tone that must have sold many newspapers, because her case overnight became a national sensation.

℞ ℟

The San Diego Union, December 1: A second article speculates that she was ruined by a man, betrayed, and abandoned—after which, in despair, she committed suicide.

The reporter interviewed a prominent physician (presumably Dr. B. F. Mertzman, who had examined the body the previous morning, Nov. 30, a half hour before the coroner's inquest, and testified later). Mertzman tells the reporter that the girl was 24 or 25 (a close age for either Lizzie Wyllie, 24, or Kate Morgan, 26). Merman states she seemed healthy, and he dismisses as 'nonsense' the idea that she was so near death from cancer that doctors had pronounced her case hopeless, as she had told Gomer[31] when the latter came to her room on Monday, Nov. 28.

Mertzman tells the reporter that the first symptoms of stomach cancer (which rarely develops under age 40, and he's never heard of one before age 35) are almost identical with the symptoms of pregnancy—pain, sourness, vomiting, as well as sallow skin. Mertzman states he cannot say for sure, but the signs point to pregnancy. He states that she appears to have been taking 'strong medicine'[32] (or 'violent medicine') to produce a miscarriage. He attributes the sallowness of her complexion and the dark rings under her eyes (mentioned by the Coronado pharmacist) as typical of such a course of self-medication.

Mertzman states "The indications are that she has already borne a child, and was [pregnant] when she died, but this cannot be definitely proven without a post-mortem examination."[33] He opines that she shot herself over "some love affair."

Mertzman references a three-hour horseback ride Lottie was said to have taken sometime after her arrival. Charles Stevens, of Star Stables, apparently saw her trying to deal with a 'fractious' horse she couldn't well control. Stevens offered to help, and she accepted, so he took her for a three-hour tour (on horseback or in a carriage). During this time she appeared to be "pleasant and companionable, if not in high spirits." In other words, for a woman suffering the terminal stage of stomach cancer, this seemed utterly out of line.

The article mentions that Lottie stopped at the Hotel Brewster after arriving in San Diego—before she ventured to Coronado and signed in at the Hotel del Coronado. At the Brewster, Lottie asked about the arrival of her presumable brother and his wife, 'Mr. and Mrs. Anderson.' Nobody by that name had signed in at the Brewster. Interestingly, she apparently did not refer to her 'brother' as Dr. Anderson, if this account is correct, but as Mr. Anderson.

ॐ ॐ

The San Francisco Chronicle reports[34] that "the [coroner's inquest] verdict was undoubtedly correct, but fails utterly to give satisfaction to the public mind since the identity of the woman is not positively fixed, and the cause of the suicide is left enveloped in mystery." The article cites "the contradictory stories told by the victim." The article dwells upon the many contradictions and inconsistencies of the saga.

Day 9—Friday, Dec. 2, 1892

The San Diego Union[35] now reports that the question of her identity is still unresolved. The paper speculates with increasing fervor that "the beautiful and mysterious stranger" killed herself over "love-trouble."

A bellman reported that Joseph E. (or A.) Jones of Boston had seen Lottie Bernard on a train, in the same car he was riding from Denver to Orange. He later recognized her in the Hotel del Coronado—in fact, he signed in after she did the afternoon of November 24. Jones' strange story highlights a mystery within a mystery: the Case of the Missing Day. Why did it take the woman a full day to make the two-hour train trip from Los Angeles to San Diego?

Jones was never called to testify at the coroner's inquest. He told the unspecified bellman that he had not mentioned the sighting on the train before, because he was loath to testify before the coroner's jury. According to Jones, he started becoming aware of the woman he would later know as Lottie Bernard, in the company of a well-dressed gentleman. People in the car began to notice "high words and bitter quarreling." This went on for some time, rising and falling. In the final minutes of the quarrel, she repeatedly begged him to forgive her for something. He adamantly and angrily refused, and stormed off the train. Jones thought nothing more of it until he saw her at the Hotel del Coronado, and he recognized her as the woman on the train. [The article uses the language "saw her at Hotel del Coronado day or so afterward"—thus, this incident could have happened either on the afternoon of November 23 after she said goodbye to the L.A. Grants in Los Angeles, or on November 24, presumably in the morning, before she completed the trip to San Diego.]

The article goes on to say that people felt her trip to San Diego was "an escapade," because she arrived without baggage. [Those people may not have been aware of the three trunks she said were being kept for her at the baggage office of the train terminal.] People noted the familiarity with which she spoke of Los Angeles hotels, which made it sound as if she were from the region.

[Employees at the Hotel del Coronado were quoted in an article in *The San Francisco Chronicle*, Dec. 6., as saying she seemed to be quite familiar with hotels in San Francisco (the Palace) and Los Angeles (the Nadeau, the Westminster) than would be expected from a common bookbindery worker only a few weeks out of Detroit.[36]]

Lottie stated that her mother and father lived in Detroit, and that G. L. Allen—the Iowa bank officer she told Gomer to wire for funds—was in charge of her finances.

The article cites puzzlement at the many contradictions in her story. It mentions that, at one point, she tipped a bellman a dollar (a day's wages) and waved it off, saying she had plenty of money—yet she had only $20 in her purse.

At this point there is speculation that G. L. Allen (who never did reply to the information about her suicide) was romantically involved with her, and had possibly "sent her away."

The article offers another speculation—that the man on the train was not her 'brother,' as she had claimed, but her lover, and that he deserted her at Orange.

The article reiterates that she gave her 'brother's' name as W. C. or M. C. Anderson of Minneapolis [in another account it was Indianapolis], but the Minneapolis directory contains no such person.

As of December 2, the 'Beautiful Stranger' remained unidentified. She was still known only as Mrs. Lottie Anderson Bernard.

Day 10—Saturday, Dec. 3, 1892

The San Diego Union reports a significant break. San Diego Police Chief Joseph W. Brenning[37] received a telegram from Miss May Wyllie of Detroit. Miss Wyllie requested a full description of the body, and asked if she had short hair, a black corset, large black hat, and gold buckle. Deputy Coroner Stetson said it was not an exact match, but it was the only communication the city had so far received about the decedent.

San Diego police, on a separate note, had telegraphed the Farmers' and Merchants' Bank in Hamburg, Iowa, for information about the elusive Mr. G. L. Allen who had wired $25 credit to Gomer on Lottie's behalf the day she died.

Police also located three trunks at the D Street baggage depot. The trunks had come from Omaha, via Denver—Denver being, we recall, the point of departure of James Jones, who told a bellman he had seen Lottie in an argument with a well-dressed man on that train. The trunks could not be opened without authorization from higher-ups in the baggage hierarchy.

Day 11—Sunday, Dec. 4, 1892

The San Diego Union identifies the dead woman as Lizzie Wyllie of Detroit. Lizzie's mother, Elizabeth Wyllie, states she is certain that the dead woman is her daughter Elizabeth 'Lizzie' Wyllie (sister of the Miss May Wyllie who the previous day telegraphed Chief Brenning to ask for details about the body).

Lizzie has relatives in San Diego, but they have not seen her since she was a child, and cannot be asked to identify her. Other relatives, it is claimed, would soon arrive from Pasadena [which never happened, as far as the history reveals] to identify her and "take care of her remains" [which also ended up not happening].

It is thus learned that Lizzie and her sister May had worked at Winn & Hammond Bookbindery in Detroit. The company was located at 12-156 Wayne Street, Tel. 220. Their foreman was a married man with children, named John G. Longfield.[38] Longfield resided at 606 12th Street, while the Wyllies (mother and two daughters; pronounced like 'Willy' or *Why-lee*) lived nearby. Apparently, Lizzie had an affair with Longfield. Soon, Lizzie, her sister May, and Longfield were all fired.

On another front, the newspaper reports that the president of the Hamburg, Iowa, bank finally responded to the telegram from San Diego Police, saying that "neither Allen nor myself know of the relatives of Mrs. Bernard. Her husband [is] supposed to be in Wichita, Kansas."

ॐ ॐ

The Los Angeles Herald reports[39] that Mrs. Elizabeth Wyllie of Detroit, upon receiving the exact description of the body as requested by her daughter May, claimed it was an exact description of Lizzie, and requested that her niece travel from Pasadena to San Diego to see the body. [No record that the niece actually did this.]

The body was described by San Diego authorities as being that of a woman five and a half feet tall, with a fair but sallow complexion. She had medium-length black hair. She had two small moles on the left cheek, broad features, high cheekbones, and brown eyes. She weighed 150 pounds, was about 26, had good teeth. She wore: a plain gold ring on the third finger of the left hand; a pure gold ring with four pearls and blue stone in its center; black corsets; and a large black hat.

ॐ ॐ

The San Francisco Chronicle reports[40] that "Driven almost to distraction by worry and shame, Mrs. Elizabeth Wyllie of Detroit admitted this afternoon that it was her daughter Lizzie who was found dead..."

Mrs. Wyllie says her daughter eloped a month earlier with [John G. Longfield] of Detroit. Neither she nor Longfield had any money. She pins the date of Lizzie's disappearance at "five weeks ago last Monday [on or about Monday, Oct. 24] she went...downtown on an errand. She never returned." She had apparently said she was going to look for work, and did not go alone.

The article reports a somewhat disjointed story that on the Saturday before Lizzie's disappearance, one afternoon a man called at the Wyllie house to tell everyone goodbye. He said he was going south, likely to California, and he 'jocosely' told May Wyllie "I will be picking roses in California while your feet are freezing in Detroit."

Mrs. Wyllie is described as 'prepossessing' and Lizzie was 'an attractive girl.'

Apparently the name L. Anderson Bernard reminded her of her lost daughter. The initial L could stand for Lizzie, while Anderson is the name of her married sister in Grand Rapids.

Regarding her receipt of the telegram describing the dead woman in Coronado, the article reads: "Mrs. Wyllie read the telegram as far as the mention of the two moles and then the paper dropped from her hands. 'My Lizzie; it's my Lizzie,' she sobbed repeatedly. 'What will become of me?' Not a word of reproach came from her lips upon the name of the dead girl."

John Longfield, her supervisor at the bookbindery, has a wife and two children. Mrs. Longfield says her husband has found work in Cleveland, and that is why he has not been home in five weeks.

Day 12—Monday, Dec. 5, 1892

The San Diego Union reports that the body is now lying in state at Johnson & Company funeral home. Many curious people are coming to look at it, "including many ladies."

The bank president in Hamburg, Iowa telegraphed to say he thought Mrs. Bernard's husband was named John. He had personally never met this John.

The paper says that a relative of Lizzie Wyllie was due to arrive on the night train from Pasadena to identify the body. [There is no indication whether or not this came to pass].

Day 13—Tuesday, Dec. 6, 1892

The San Diego Union claims[41] that it is now for certain that the dead girl is 'pretty Lizzie Wyllie' of Detroit.

The article claims that she 'disappeared' from her home 'some six weeks ago' [which would put it in October or even as far back as September, depending on how reliable the reporter's story was].

The paper notes that Lizzie's Pasadena relative "has not yet materialized."

Authorities contacted a Mr. John Bernard of Wichita to inform him his wife "had suicided," to which he chose not to respond.

The love affair of Lizzie Wyllie and John G. Longfield is being fleshed out in the voracious press. Apparently, the two lovers were so obvious that it caused a scandal. Despite knowing he was married, Lizzie continued going with him.

After being fired, Lizzie visited her married sister, Mrs. [Louisa] Anderson, in Grand Rapids, Michigan for a time, and then returned home [to her mother and sister] for a short time six weeks earlier, before then 'disappearing.' It is assumed this accounts for the dead woman having several handkerchiefs marked 'Lottie Anderson.'

Mrs. Elizabeth Wyllie was certain the dead girl was her daughter Lizzie. For one thing, the dead girl had two moles on her left cheek, as did Lizzie.

Speculation has it that "Longfield was at Hamburg under an assumed name, and sent Lizzie the $25. If this be the case, who came to California with her, with whom did she have a quarrel at Orange, and who as the man that left her at that point? Who was the dead girl expecting at Hotel del Coronado? Not a brother, but one Longfield, if the truth were known, Allen of Hamburg may have played a leading part in the dastardly affair himself. Longfield is known at Detroit as a sport, and a rounder of not the best reputation even for one of his class."

The paper mentions that Lizzie continues lying in the funeral home, looking peaceful as if sleeping at home. Mrs. Wyllie is expected to send word on what to do with the body. The three trunks at the San Diego baggage depot remain unclaimed.

The San Francisco Chronicle reports[42] that staff at the Hotel del Coronado were impressed with the charm, education, and class of the woman who died at the hotel. They feel her knowledge of the fine hotels of San Francisco and Los Angeles could not be forthcoming from a factory girl only recently run away from Detroit.

In a separate article, the same paper reports that Mrs. Longfield sent her husband a letter in Cleveland on Saturday [Dec. 3]. Not knowing his address, she sent it General Delivery. She had a reply from him this morning, saying "I received a letter from Miss Wyllie last Wednesday [Nov. 30]. Will send it on at once. There is no truth in it."

Day 14—Wednesday, Dec. 7, 1892

The San Diego Union reports[43] that the undertaker has sent a photograph of the dead woman's face to Mrs. Wyllie in Detroit. In so doing, the mortuary noted an apparent discrepancy that Lizzie had pierced ears, whereas the corpse did not.

It was reported that the handkerchiefs did not read 'Lottie Anderson,' as previously reported, but 'Louisa Anderson'—the name of Lizzie's aunt [previously referenced as her married sister] in Grand Rapids, Michigan.

The article mentions that a telegram had come [sender not named] the previous day, Dec. 6, swinging the weight back into the Bernard camp. Evidently, a professional gambler named L. A. Bernard had come through Hamburg recently. This man was now thought to be the deceased's husband. Bernard was said to have left Hamburg November 7 for Topeka, Kansas. He had said his wife was sick in California, and he was going to bring her back to Iowa. He tried to borrow money for the trip, but could not get a loan and has not been heard from since. G. L. Allen of Hamburg, who wired the $25 credit, is said to have been a roommate of Bernard in Illinois. Allen never met Bernard's wife, but contributed the $25 out of charity. The message concludes by restating a strong belief that the identification of the body as Lizzie Wyllie's is wrong, implying that she was, after all, Mrs. Bernard.

In San Diego, the Bernard story is being discredited by the newspapers. The papers follow an even more confusing track. They imply that Allen was romantically linked with the dead woman, and invented the sick wife story 'as a blind.' They claim that a San Diego man, who knows Allen, says Allen is a wealthy cattleman and ladies' man. The papers opine that "either Allen is a consummate liar and had dealings with Miss Lizzie

Wyllie, which he is trying to conceal, or the girl...is Mrs. L. A. Bernard"
[presumably the wife of the L. A. Bernard reported by G. L. Allen].

❧ ❦

The San Francisco Chronicle opines[44] that Miss Lizzie Wyllie of Detroit
and Mrs. L. Anderson Bernard "were not the same person. The Wyllie girl
is alive and well in Toronto and Mrs. Bernard is supposed to have been the
wife of a Hamburg, Iowa gambler..."

"...As he promised in his dispatch of yesterday, Longfield, whose name
has been associated with Miss Wyllie's disappearance, enclosed to his wife
a letter from Miss Wyllie, dated Toronto, in which she says that she is not
coming home... and indicates that Lizzie left home on account of trouble
with her family."

Day 15—Thursday, Dec. 8, 1892

The San Diego Union reports[45] that, based on the issue of the pierced
ears, the dead woman was not Lizzie Wyllie. Lizzie had pierced ears and
wore silver earrings, while the dead woman's ears were not pierced.

G. L. Allen of Hamburg, Iowa, is again reported as saying he had been a
schoolmate of a gambler named L. A. Bernard, whose wife lay ill in
California. At her request [i.e., Gomer's] he wired $25 credit, without ever
having met her. The San Diego papers, however, tend to be suspicious of
Allen and not believe his story because of details that in themselves are
convoluted and questionable.

A Mrs. Florence S. Howard, of Orange, California, writes that the dead
woman is one Josie Brown, 24, of Detroit. Josie Brown had stayed with
Mrs. Howard during the previous summer. She said Josie Brown had a
sister named Mrs. Anderson. A young man claiming to be her brother, and
calling himself Dr. Brown, of Detroit, had spent some time there, but
claimed to have come from Minneapolis."

The paper reports that the three trunks remain as yet unopened at the
baggage depot.

❧ ❦

The Los Angeles Times reports[46] that "young woman's trunk and
baggage are...at Mrs. [L.A.] Grant's, No. 917 South Hill Street, where she
was last seen. When she left, on the 23rd...she stated that she would be back
in time for Thanksgiving dinner, but not a word has been heard from her
since."

The story relates that she arrived from Omaha about two months earlier [September or October]. She said her husband was a gambler, and she did not know what had become of him.

She applied at several employment agencies. She first found work as a domestic at the R. M. Widneys', and then at the T. H. Hughes'. Lastly, she found employment at the L. A. Grants'.

The day before she left Los Angeles, she was anxious to get some papers signed, and appeared to be very worried about something.

She wore the ring and the black underclothes found on the body in Coronado. She had two moles on her left cheek.

"She told several persons that her name was Lizzie, but that she liked the name of Kittie better, and that was the reason she adopted it."

The paper reported that she came to Los Angeles from San Francisco. She was "well posted" in San Francisco, and knew all about the public places and the hotels, which shows she must have lived there.

While in Los Angeles, she maintained an excellent reputation. She kept to her duties, never went out at night, and had no men about. She seemed to be in good spirits on the day she left for San Diego, and "promised faithfully that she would be home next day in time to cook the Thanksgiving dinner."

She appeared to be 'fairly well educated' and had traveled much, since her husband was a gambler.

The Evening Express (Los Angeles) reports that "The woman, whose husband was a gambler, was described as being very pretty."

                      ઌ ઌ

The San Francisco Chronicle reports[47] that it is believed the suicide is Mrs. Katie Logan, a domestic for several families in Los Angeles. She came from Omaha about two months ago [late September or early October]. The description of the dead woman fits her exactly. "It is believed that Mrs. Logan also lived in San Francisco, since she was well informed about that city."

Day 16—Friday, Dec. 9, 1892

The San Diego Union reports[48] that the dead woman is still unidentified. The feeling now is that she was not Lizzie Wyllie, who is said to be living with her lover John G. Longfield in Ontario, Canada. She is now thought to be the wife of Iowa gambler L. A. Bernard.

Los Angeles Police Chief Glass has informed San Diego Police Chief Brenning that the dead woman was probably a missing housemaid from Los Angeles, named Katie Logan.

The newspaper also raises, perhaps for the first time, the name Kate Morgan that will receive most of the press attention in the case spanning at least three centuries. The paper connects the dots thus: "...Mrs. Bernard is really the woman's name...she was at Orange last year under the name of Josie Brown...she was at Omaha two months ago, where she perhaps met Allen of Hamburg...came to Los Angeles under the name of Kate Morgan, and appeared [in San Diego] under her real name [Lottie A. Bernard]."

↾ ↽

The Los Angeles Times reports[49] that the trunk of Kate Morgan was moved, on order of Los Angeles Police Chief Glass, to the central police station from Contractor Grant's house.

The trunk was opened there, and it was found that her home was in Hamburg, Iowa. This was the town from which the Hotel del Coronado received the wire of $25 credit.

A marriage certificate indicated she was married to Thomas E. Morgan by Rev. W. H. Howes, on 30 December 1885. Her maiden name was Miss Katie K. Farmer.

Telegrams between Chief Glass in Los Angeles and Chief Brenning in San Diego indicated the body still lay unclaimed at Johnson & Company mortuary on Fifth Street in San Diego.

Mr. Grant stated he never had a better servant in his house. When she went missing, he immediately reported it to police.

↾ ↽

The Los Angeles Herald reports[50] that the trunk marked 'Mrs. Kate Morgan' was taken from the L. A. Grants' home to the Los Angeles police station.

The box contained a tin box marked 'Louise' [or 'Louisa'?].

There was a photograph of a man about 50 years old, with a full beard, tinged with gray. On the reverse side of this picture was a name (scratched out) but the word Visalia left visible.

There was a photograph of a man about 35 years old, with a black mustache, black hair, and thick skull, "who looked something like a sporting character." The reporter speculates that this might be "her husband, who had deserted her."

There were photographs of two boys, about 9 and 10; a girl about 2; and a baby.

On several photos, names had been "carefully erased."

There was a paper containing a lock of blonde hair. On the paper someone had written in a coarse hand, "Elizabeth A. Morgan's hair."

A letter from W. J. [W.T.] Farmer, Hanford, recommended Mrs. Morgan as an honorable and trustworthy woman.

The trunk contained the cards of several ladies and their addresses, where most likely Kate Morgan [Katie Logan] had worked: Mrs. J. H. McDonough of San Rafael; Mrs. M. R. Abbott of San Francisco; and Mrs. Ottinger of San Francisco.

A 'cabinet size photo' shows Mrs. Morgan "as a woman about 26, with black eyes, large ears, a rather large, open face, and somewhat coarse features." It seemed to be a recent picture. In the reporter's judgment, the photo doesn't represent a woman accustomed to staying in fine hotels, or wears lace shawls. She doesn't seem pretty, and her features don't look like those of an educated woman.

ɂ’Ʉ’ ☔

The San Francisco Chronicle reports[51] that the dead woman was undoubtedly Kate Morgan...

"Her maiden name was Katie K. Farmer. She had only been on the coast for two months, and, as near as can be learned, she worked for W. T. Farmer, a supposed relative, at Hanford, Tulare County."

Day 17—Saturday, Dec. 10, 1892

The San Diego Union reports that the trunk of the woman in Los Angeles [Katie Logan, a pseudonym] was opened. The owner of the trunk has been identified, based on papers and photos inside, as Kate Morgan. She and Lottie A. Bernard are thought to be one and the same.

Inside the trunk was found a tin box with the name 'Louisa Anderson' on it. That name matches the name embroidered on the handkerchiefs found in the dead woman's room at the Hotel del Coronado. The effects include a lock of hair. *The Los Angeles Herald* says that a photograph of Mrs. Morgan does not match the description of the Coronado suicide. This is contradicted by other evidence, including a marriage certificate dated December 30, 1885, for Thomas E. Morgan and Kate K. Farmer, united in matrimony by Rev. W. E. Howe in Hamburg, Iowa.

This article states that [Katie Logan] had been a domestic servant in the home of the L. A. Grants, a family of Los Angeles. Her employers and co-workers described her as 'reticent' about her life, saying only she was married to a gambler and was unhappy about it.

Echoing a report in *The Los Angeles Times*, *The San Diego Union* says [Katie Logan] had been in California for two months. She had previously worked for a W. T. Farmer [Kate Morgan's uncle, in Hanford, California, near Visalia]. Police believe Kate Morgan had gone from Chicago to

Omaha, and from there to Cheyenne, Ogden, Sacramento, and then Hanford. In Hanford, she had gotten a letter of recommendation from W. T. Farmer. Then she had traveled to Los Angeles.

The paper opines that the contents of the trunk—in which all names, addresses, and other personal information had been destroyed—made it evident that she wanted to conceal her identity.[52]

Mr. Farmer has been contacted for information.

Day 18—Sunday, Dec. 11, 1892

The San Diego Union reports[53] that a Mr. A. D. Swarts of Los Angeles had contacted the coroner's office in San Diego to say that he had known her since 1869. He says she is [Kate Morgan], the granddaughter of a miller named Joe Chandler in Riverton, Iowa [near Hamburg]. Swarts says that Tom Morgan, Sr., her husband's rich uncle, lives in that area, along with other wealthy relatives, all of whom would help her have a decent burial. Accordingly, San Diego authorities sent telegrams to several of these persons.

The paper reports that large numbers of visitors, mostly female, daily throng to Johnson & Company funeral parlor to view the body.

The three trunks at the San Diego baggage depot have been claimed "by the owners" and this removes "any remaining doubt" that the dead woman was Mrs. Kate Morgan.

Day 19—Monday, Dec. 12, 1892

The San Diego Union reports[54] that Kate's grandfather, Joe Chandler, of Riverton, Iowa, sent a telegram to the undertaker, Johnson & Company of San Diego. "Your telegram received regarding Kate Morgan, *née* Farmer. Bury her and send me statement.—J. W. Chandler."

The newspaper says that "none of her other relatives have uttered a word." The cause of her suicide is still unknown.

The paper says "she will be buried today." [In fact, her funeral was not held until two days later, Dec. 14, followed by her burial].

&ntml; ❧ ❧

The Los Angeles Times on [date uncertain, but after Dec. 10] comments[55] on the report from W. T. Farmer, Kate Morgan's uncle at Hanford, California, that she had considerable money with her when she arrived at his residence. Kate said she intended to deposit the money in a bank. Farmer opined that Kate was frugal, and had employment while in Los

Angeles, and thus would not have spent her money. This was in reaction to comments that she died with only $16 in her purse.

Day 20—Tuesday, Dec. 13, 1892

No news.

Day 21—Wednesday, Dec. 14, 1892 (Funeral and Burial)

According to *The San Diego Union*,[56] the funeral was held at 10:00 a.m. at Johnson & Company. A Rev. H. B. Restarick officiated with prayers and Bible verses. Members of the Brotherhood of St. Andrew, along with ladies of the Episcopal Church, made responses during the service. The funeral was well attended. After the funeral, the casket was put in a hearse and carried to Mount Hope Cemetery for burial.

The Daily Bee, San Diego [story apparently dated Dec. 13] reports that there were "many women" at the funeral. "Prominent ladies sent flowers for the casket, but no one followed the remains to the cemetery."

                                            ∾ *∾*

The Los Angeles Times reports[57] that W. T. Farmer, Kate Morgan's uncle in Hanford, California, finally responded to Los Angeles Police Chief Glass' inquiries. Farmer says Kate had no cause for suicide, and implies that, if the body was indeed hers, something else caused her death. He wrote that her husband, Thomas E. Morgan (Tom Morgan) was traveling[58] on business for a manufacturing company, and his home is in Hamburg, Iowa. Farmer had known them for many years. Kate wrote to Farmer from Los Angeles, saying she had secured work with the Whitney family. She had a good sum of money with her when she stayed with Farmer in Hanford. She had one flat-top trunk, two leather satchels, and a lady's gold watch, and said she would deposit the money in a bank.

Farmer enumerates some of her relatives—Henry Broomback and Thomas Morgan of Hamburg, Iowa; her grandfather, Joe W. Chandler, and John Samuella, of Riverton, Iowa—and continues to protest he does not believe Kate Morgan would have committed suicide, and perhaps there is a mistake about the identity pinned on the corpse.

The reporter presses his own conviction that there can be no doubt it was Kate Morgan, and that she did commit suicide, and in fact left the L.A. Grants with that intention already in mind. However, the reporter goes on to say that a number of mysteries about the case may never be answered— what happened to the considerable sum of money Farmer said she left Hanford with; what papers she was so anxious to have signed; and why she killed herself. The article affirms that Kate Morgan's relatives paid for the burial in San Diego.

ℂ ℃

The body of the unknown woman—Lottie A. Bernard? Josie Brown? Katie Logan? Kate Morgan? Lizzie Wyllie?—lay in state several weeks at the mortuary. The funeral was variously reported as having been held either Tuesday, December 13, or the 9th, or even the 15th. Many ladies attended the funeral. Many people sent flowers, but none accompanied the casket to Mount Hope Cemetery. Pious, overwrought ladies in Sunday finery trooped daily from dawn to dusk to the funeral parlor, with its smells of flowers and candle wax. A High-Church funeral followed, in the best Episcopalian tradition. The simple coffin was loaded on a donkey cart, and the dead woman rumbled off without a single pall bearer or mourner, outside town to a forgotten grave at Mt. Hope Cemetery, Market Street. Neither the relatives of Lizzie Wyllie, nor those of Kate Morgan, ever showed up. Kate Morgan's grandfather paid the bill, with only the telegraphed words: "Bury her and send me the bill." He knew his granddaughter all too well.

Her uncle, W. T. Farmer of Hanford, the last family member to see Kate Morgan, said she was happy, had no cause for suicide, and was married to Thomas Morgan who "has been traveling in the interest of some manufacturing company." Kate must have really pulled the wool over her uncle's eyes. Joe Chandler must have been ashamed of her, and kept the truth from Farmer—that Kate was a source of constant trouble. Farmer says Kate was traveling with a single trunk—not three trunks, as reported in Los Angeles. The three trunks belonged to Lizzie, and were part of the switch the two women pulled. Farmer stated he thought authorities were mistaken in identifying the corpse as Kate's—as I believe they were.

Part IV. Solved!

The Core of My Theory

Key Points

In a moment, we are going to rewind the timeline traced in "Part III: What We Know For Sure," and re-examine the details in a new light. First, let me summarize my theory.

Blackmail was the real reason: Traditionally, no reason is usually offered for Lottie A. Bernard's appearance at the Hotel del Coronado. Less often, the story goes that she had been abandoned by her partner in crime—allegedly her husband, Tom Morgan who used her charms to lure men in to card games on trains, only to get them drunk and rob them—and that Tom had no use for her anymore when she got pregnant. In the latter scenario, Tom would be the 'brother,' a 'Dr. Anderson,' about whom she frequently and desperately inquired at the hotel's front desk. Supposedly, then, she killed herself out of despair. Even more rarely, the story goes that she was murdered, either by Tom, or by shadowy and powerful men of the region—one thinks immediately of John Spreckels, one of the wealthiest men in the United States, and the most powerful by far in the San Diego region. While the facts do not support any of these theories, John Spreckels is in fact the key to the entire saga. He is the biggest puzzle piece, and all the pieces start to neatly and logically snap into place when we consider one huge detail: John Spreckels had recently become sole owner of the Hotel del Coronado.

I believe John Spreckels was the target of a blackmail plot to extort money from him in a false claim of paternity.

Two women, not one: The traditional story has it that only one person was involved—Kate Morgan, a con artist and grifter from Hamburg, Iowa. The evidence clearly shows there were two women and up to two men involved.

Lizzie Wyllie, not Kate Morgan: Where the traditional story has it that the woman who died was Kate Morgan, I believe the dead woman was Elizabeth 'Lizzie' Wyllie (pronounced like Wylie, of which it is a variant. The body was first identified as being that of Lottie A. Bernard, the fictitious name under which she registered. Days later, the body was identified as that of Lizzie Wyllie. A few days after that, based on an anonymous tip, police shifted their attention to a woman named Kate Morgan. The change in IDs was arbitrary and based largely on the flimsy factor of pierced ears.

Two men, not one: The traditional story has it that a man was in the background, usually considered to be Kate's husband Tom Morgan. I believe there were two men in the background—one of them John G. Longfield, Lizzie's married lover with whom she fled Detroit after she became pregnant; and probably Kate's husband or a male lover.

Web of Indirect Evidence

I don't have direct proof or a smoking gun to prove my theory that it was blackmail, being perpetrated by Kate Morgan and three accomplices (Lizzie Wyllie, John G. Longfield, and possibly Tom Morgan or another lover of Kate's). There is not, for example, let us say, a hypothetical telegram from Kate Morgan to John Spreckels, threatening him and demanding money. There is currently no such document, nor is there even known to have been one, though I suspect it was how Kate Morgan conveyed her message to Spreckels as she got Lizzie ('Lottie A. Bernard') situated at Spreckels' hotel. Logically, the timing may have been that Spreckels knew of her on or before the day she checked in.

Once we start sifting through all the clues, they form a network of corroborating and circumstantial evidence so strong that one begins to approach certainty. Every piece of the puzzle makes sense once the whole thing is assembled. There are no loose ends left, and that makes this at least a strong theory—and it may well be possible to find other stray granules of fact that have drifted around in the wind, disconnected, for over a century, once people know where to look.

We have here what could be called a brittle case. It is a cold case in the truest sense—the Victorian era is long gone, all the witnesses are dead, key evidence was tampered with and lost, and even the official transcript of the coroner's inquest was lost for a time (its integrity therefore compromised). Still, using the voluminous evidence compiled by the Heritage Department, and other facts gathered from library and internet sources, it is possible to formulate a theory or strong conjecture that is compelling in how all of its myriad pieces fit together.

It is a complicated story—some would say far-fetched, but one has only to look at the contorted and amazing manner in which Kate Morgan lived her life to lay aside all disbelief and doubt. Here was a woman who traveled throughout the Central and Western United States leaving a trail of aliases. Her life itself, and that of the fictitious 'brother' who keeps shadowing her in parallel under ever-changing names, is like a huge fantasy story that she wove, using the transcontinental railroad and her dark and hyper-active imagination as a loom.

Rewinding the Tape

Day 0—Wednesday, Nov. 23, 1892 (Katie Logan in L.A.)

It may seem strange that I did not choose to start the timeline on Thanksgiving Day, Nov. 24, when Lottie A. Bernard sprang into life. Day Zero may seem like an odd choice also, but it is a ghostly nod to the last day in the short life of an imaginary person named Mrs. Katie Logan. And this is a highly important part of our story, because Los Angeles Police unearthed some startling, major clues in her trunk during the nationwide search for the phantom housemaid. Katie Logan appeared out of Omaha (coincidentally the capital of the state in which Tom Morgan would live most of his life; and also about fifty miles from Kate Morgan's home town of Hamburg, Iowa). Katie existed for thirty to sixty days, during which she worked as a domestic temp in three prominent Los Angeles households. She was attractive, efficient, and well-liked. Her last employers, the civil contractor L. A. Grant and his wife, heartily invited her to return from some unspecified errands that afternoon, and to assist the family with their Thanksgiving dinner. We know, of course, that she vanished, never to be seen again, and the Grants missed her enough to report her disappearance almost immediately to Los Angeles Police. Thus, even as a new fictional person (Lottie A. Bernard) sprang to life in the Cities of Coronado and San Diego some two hours south as the train chugs, the LAPD was already developing a missing person's case on Katie Logan.

LAPD's case pursued the usual lawful ends, but was headed on a trajectory that would soon coincide with the Lottie A. Bernard suicide investigation in the San Diego area. The critical element at the end of that trajectory, a critical element in the case—and in this theory—was a single trunk containing the possessions of the missing domestic. The Grants said Katie Logan had brought the trunk with her from Omaha, her reputed last residence. At the end of the trajectory, that trunk would be taken to police headquarters in Los Angeles. Until the police had reasonable cause, they could not lawfully open the trunk—anymore than San Diego Police were able to open Lottie's three trunks at the baggage depot there. However, when the missing Katie Logan of Los Angeles was connected to the dead Lottie A. Bernard of Coronado, police did open the trunk. Inside, they found a wealth of artifacts that baffled them, and have continued to baffle analysts until now. The contents of that trunk are remarkable, because they contain artifacts belonging to both Kate Morgan and Lizzie Wyllie. This trunk connects the two women. It connects them not only in some vague manner, but *in situ*, in the location of one of Kate Morgan's notorious and enigmatic false identities. The trunk is not the only connection—Deputy Coroner Stetson found hankies belonging to Lizzie's aunt in the dead woman's room at the Hotel Del.

As we noted in the previous part, Katie Logan made that strange statement to another domestic—a statement so baffling that it can only be truthful, amid the often dubious claims and reports of the Yellow Press. Katie Logan was described as being quiet and keeping to herself. She was worried about several things. She was unhappily married to a gambler, and did not know his whereabouts. She was anxious to have some unspecified papers signed, but nobody learned what these were about. Then, another woman working as a domestic stated that Katie Logan informed her that her name was Lizzie, but that she preferred Kittie or Katie. Katie Logan (who is usually suspected of being Kate Morgan) actually tells another domestic that her name is Lizzie. This, like the trunk, ties the two women together. And if Katie Logan was really Lizzie Wyllie, this supports my theory (borne out by other evidence) that Lottie Bernard was Lizzie.

One can imagine a brief conversation—later reported to Los Angeles police detectives—between two domestics in the shadowed halls of the wealthy Grant home. One can imagine how the pseudonymous Katie Logan lets her guard down and blurts out, "My name is really Lizzie," and then she catches herself, realizing her *faux pas*, and quickly recovers by adding: "...but I prefer Kittie...err, Katie...so I go by that name."

Finally, some hankies belonging to Lizzie Wyllie (actually, her Aunt Louisa) turned up in that same trunk.

Lizzie Wyllie was an attractive but air-headed young Detroit woman in serious trouble. She had gotten pregnant by her married lover, John Longfield, with whom she ran away to California after they were both fired from the bookbinding plant (Bin & Hammond) where they worked. She had relatives in San Diego, but did not visit with them.[59]

Now why would Katie Logan's trunk show up in the L.A. Grants' house, with articles in them belonging to both Kate Morgan and Lizzie Wyllie? Remember that Lottie A. Bernard at the Hotel del Coronado was telling people she had three trunks sitting at the freight depot in San Diego. She could not check those trunks out, because her 'brother' (most people until now have thought that was Tom Morgan; I believe it was John Longfield) stormed off the train with the tickets in his pocket at Orange. Those three trunks disappeared—which appeared to resolve yet another issue. But it seems far-fetched to think of the coincidence that (a) Lottie Bernard said she couldn't get her three trunks out and (b) the police actually determined there were three trunks at the depot but, as with the trunk in Los Angeles, they couldn't open them. This simple element is a good example of the tissue of fine details that combine to form a tenable theory in this old, brittle, cold case. We have Lottie in Coronado, stating repeatedly to various persons that she had three trunks in the depot in San Diego, but she didn't have the claim checks (with numbers on them); and there actually were exactly three trunks (not two, not four) sitting unclaimed at the depot during that precise time period—with tags on them, but no name and no matching claim checks with numbers to redeem the trunks. This tends to corroborate Lottie's story.

By the time the San Diego Police felt free to open the trunks, the trunks had vanished. The police felt the owner had picked them up. I suspect they were taken away under false pretenses by either the Spreckels Machine or by Kate Morgan and her accomplices. Since John Spreckels' agents controlled San Diego by then (he owned most of Coronado, much of downtown San Diego, the newspapers, the utilities, the rail system, the water flume, and anything else that was for sale) it is more likely that the Spreckels Machine removed the three trunks from play. The Spreckels Machine would have seen its core interest as protecting their master from scandal, at a critical time when he and his father were lobbying the President and Congress to prevent the overthrow of the Hawai'ian monarchy and therefore the loss of Spreckels' vast sugar fortune. We must remember, too, that San Diego had only a rudimentary police force at this time. Chief Brenning was a recent successor to the first chief, Coyne, who took office in 1889. San Diego had no detective force, and it is almost a given that a man as powerful and connected as Spreckels would be using Pinkertons or a similar agency, perhaps even his own private detective force. Thus Spreckels' private law enforcement arm would be far more sophisticated than Chief Branding's uniformed patrol.

If we believe that the three trunks in San Diego were really those of the woman at the Hotel del Coronado (Lottie Bernard), and if we believe, as I do, that Lottie Bernard was really Lizzie Wyllie, then we may presume that Lizzie brought three trunks out of Detroit. We know Lizzie was a snappy and stylish dresser, so it's hard to imagine she did not travel with a wardrobe. As much as the three trunks were Lizzie's, the single trunk at the L.A. Grants' house was Kate Morgan's trunk.

But if we believe that Lizzie first played Katie Logan in Los Angeles, and then played Lottie Bernard in Coronado, what is the meaning of this? How did Lizzie Wyllie, pretending to be the fictitious Katie Logan, have in her possession Kate Morgan's single trunk? Because Kate Morgan and her lover—presumably her husband, Tom Morgan, though there is room to believe she had abandoned her husband at that point and had another lover, who was the second man in Hamburg, setting up a $25 credit line for Lottie Bernard at the Hotel del Coronado—were training Lizzie for the hoped-for big coup in Coronado. Helping out was Lizzie's lover, John Longfield, who must have traveled to Hamburg with the other man to set up the credit line that came through on the day of Lottie Bernard's death.

On the topic of the trunks for one more moment: it makes sense that Kate Morgan had one trunk, because she was a frequent traveler and (as evidenced from the photos inside the trunk in Los Angeles) not a very good looking woman, nor a snappy dresser. On the other hand, Lizzie was a beautiful young woman with fine clothing, as witnesses said of Lottie A. Bernard. Lizzie had fine tastes in clothes, and it makes sense she would have eloped with three trunks—probably full of fine dresses and hats and purses and so forth. She may have been poor after losing her job, and she probably pawned her silver earrings, as we'll see later, but a woman like this would give her life to avoid being ill-dressed.

Kate Morgan is known to have spent time in San Francisco, where the Spreckels family had their estates and business headquarters. LAPD found, in her trunk, calling cards of a number of wealthy ladies there, although not of any Spreckels family members that we know of. I believe Kate Morgan was in the business of traveling around the country, finding temporary domestic work in wealthy homes, and setting up all manner of scams, as one can deduce from her many aliases. While in San Francisco, she would most certainly have learned all the gossip and inside news about wealthy families there from her fellow domestics. Ever one to exploit any possibility for a con job or a blackmail opportunity, it seems she came to focus on John Spreckels as the perfect target for the largest and most daring scam of her life. All this is conjecture, in itself, and would not stand up to the light of day on its own, but follows from many other fine details known for certain, and from minute conjectures that can be more solidly drawn. An example is that of Katie Logan blurting out that her real name is Lizzie, but she quickly catches herself and says that she goes by Kittie or Katie because she likes that name better—probably stammering, the poor airhead, at that moment unable to remember even her fake name.

I believe that Kate Morgan probably learned of some true life dalliance of John Spreckels, and embroidered it to fit her plan. The distance from San Francisco to San Diego would be enough to gain her the breathing space, in that age before rapid transit, to threaten Spreckels, and to collect the hush money and disappear before anyone could come down to investigate. She also knew Spreckels owned the Hotel del Coronado, the most remote of his possessions, on an island off the coast yet. That is why she chose his hotel to stage her crime.

We know that Detroit is mentioned in the travels of Kate and Tom. At one point, she refers to her 'brother' as being Doctor So-and-So of Detroit. It is logical to think she met Lizzie Wyllie either in Detroit, or immediately after Lizzie and John Longfield left Detroit for California—in the latter case, most likely on a train. Lizzie was pregnant—for the second time, again out of wedlock (because Dr. Mertzman was to testify at the Coroner's Inquest that the dead woman was most likely pregnant, that she had borne a child before, and that she was taking extreme measures to induce a miscarriage). It is easy to fit together the pieces logically then. If Kate Morgan could create the impression that a domestic servant or other lover had become pregnant by him—if she could even imply that—and the threat was staged in a locale far removed from San Francisco, then Kate was gambling that Spreckels or his agents would accept some kind of written release in return for hush money.

I mentioned earlier that Katie Logan came from Omaha, Nebraska, which is about fifty miles from Kate's home town of Hamburg, Iowa. It seems that Kate, in training the rather slow Lizzie, had to use aliases and details the poor girl could remember. Thus, 'Katie' was easy to remember as a version of Kate, the experienced name-changer, and Logan was similar to Morgan. She might have drilled Lizzie and helped her to remember her fictitious name—*if you forget, just think of my name,* Kate Morgan probably told her, *and you'll easily remember your name is Katie Logan.* We know from the other pseudonyms that Kate always had a doctor-brother floating around, from some city picked at a whim. This time, the fictitious doctor-brother was going to be Dr. M.C. or M.E. Anderson (Lizzie's aunt Louisa's last name) of Detroit (Lizzie's home town). Kate probably picked a city from her own reference (Omaha) for Katie Logan's home town. There was no doctor-brother for Katie, as far as we know—keeping things simple during the training wheels stage. And when it came to Lottie A. Bernard, one has to suspect that the very name Kate Morgan chose for Lizzie to bear must have some trigger effect on Spreckels. Kate had worked among the wealthy homes of San Francisco, and could easily have heard gossip of any extramarital liaisons John Spreckels might have had with his servants. Kate might even have purchased some telltale letters from a fellow servant who had such an affair with her employer—all guesswork—and this could have been the stack of letters or papers Lottie A. Bernard was burning in her fireplace in Room 302 the day before her death. Maybe Spreckels' real lover was a woman with a name like Charlotte Bernard, as I have it in the dramatization later in this book. A blackmail note from Lottie Bernard, couched in just the right wording, would have gone over the heads of Spreckels' secretaries, but would surely have shot his eyebrows up and sent shivers up and down his spine. We will never know exactly how Kate Morgan planned to pull off her scheme. Most likely, the incriminating letters were all burned in Room 302 on November 28, 1892, and the blackmail message soon after conveniently destroyed by Spreckels' unknown chief of private security.

Kate Morgan did not understand into what a hornet's nest, what a nightmare, she was leading her accomplices. Spreckels was at that moment in Washington, lobbying with the President and Congress, and hardly in a position to respond to a rather absurd threat. Kate would not have realized the power of the institution Spreckels had put together in San Diego. He controlled thousands of lives, thousands of acres of land, many millions of dollars of real estate and capital equipment, and he would need an army of accountants and other functionaries to manage all this *in absentia*. Moreover, Allan Pinkerton (1819-1884) had created a unique detective and spy service. Pinkerton had served Lincoln during the Civil War, and he served many wealthy masters afterward as a strike-breaker and corporate advocate. It would be logical for a family as wealthy as the Speckles to be on intimate terms with such services. Kate Morgan had never really gone up against people of the power and wealth the Spreckels family possessed. John Spreckels was his father's trusted right-hand man, and a brilliant, ruthless businessman in his own right, with predatory instincts—see how he helped Elisha Babcock slide into debt as the economy worsened after 1888, and called the loans when it was clear Babcock could not repay them. Spreckels, although an absentee landlord (he didn't permanently move to San Diego until after the devastating San Francisco Earthquake of 1906), would have protected his San Diego possessions with a formidable array of security and intelligence—what I call the Spreckels Machine.

Kate Morgan saw the opportunity to use a pregnant and desperate Lizzie Wyllie in her scheme to blackmail Spreckels. From events that followed later, I surmise that John Longfield—a ladies' man, though he had several children and was married to a seemingly tolerant and gullible woman—had removed Lizzie from Detroit to dump her off somewhere. By Victorian standards, Lizzie was a totally ruined woman. Even her mother had reached the brink of despair over her daughter.

Kate Morgan brought Lizzie to Los Angeles and trained her in the art of impersonation. She taught her to use a false name—Katie Logan—and to accept short temp assignments (three in the month of October-November 1892 alone)—to get used to pseudonyms and falsifications. At the chosen moment—which happened to be Thanksgiving Day—Kate had Lizzie travel to San Diego to check into the Hotel del Coronado.

Day 0 ½—The Missing Day

Before we go to Day 1, we must address another major part of the mystery—'The Missing Day.' From Los Angeles to San Diego is now, and was then, about a two hour train ride. We know that Lizzie ('Katie Logan') bade the Grants farewell sometime during the daylight hours of Wednesday, November 23, and signed in at the Hotel del Coronado in the afternoon of Thursday, November 24. What did she do during these approximately twenty-four hours? A remarkable and convoluted story surfaced after her death, which opens up a breath-taking explanation.

When we examine the guest register at the Hotel del Coronado for November 24, we see that Lottie A. Bernard signs in as the eighth person on the page, of a total of twelve persons. The ninth person to sign in is one Joseph A. Jones of Boston. Jones is assigned a room on the same floor (the third floor, or top floor, which is a cheaper flight of rooms normally taken by staff and the less well-heeled, because in the era before elevators, first floor rooms were usually the more expensive and convenient). Remarkably, it comes to light in the newspapers after the Coroner's Inquest, that Jones had told an unnamed bellman he had recognized Lottie A. Bernard as a woman he saw having an argument with a man on the train from Denver.

Now consider this. If Lizzie ('Katie Logan'/'Lottie Bernard') traveled from Los Angeles to San Diego, how could she simultaneously be on a train heading west from Denver at that same exact time?

There can really only be one explanation. Lizzie was said to be very anxious during her time in Los Angeles. She was pregnant, and time was running out. The only person in the world who could help her was John Longfield—who she undoubtedly wished would leave his wife and children and marry her, which would explain the papers she was anxious to take care of in Los Angeles (probably having to do with his proposed divorce; just as likely, a ruse planted by Kate Morgan as a carrot to keep Lizzie devoted to her dangerous impersonation). We know that someone— a man—physically walked into a bank in Hamburg, Iowa, and told the bank officer he wanted to extend credit to a woman at the Hotel del Coronado. Presumably, that would have to be John Longfield, posing as G. L. Allen to pull off this feat, since Tom Morgan could not have done it without being recognized.

Now the evidence suggests that John Longfield was not anxious to leave his family. He kept up a correspondence with his wife, in which he claimed to be in Cleveland, looking for work. There is reason to think, however, that John Longfield was having an affair with Kate Morgan by now. A compelling fact is that Kate's husband, Tom Morgan, shows up in autumn

1893—less than a year after his wife's purported death—in his boyhood home in Nebraska, and marries a new bride. Tom Morgan becomes a town constable, a mail carrier, the devoted father of a daughter and lifelong spouse of his new wife, and a deacon in his church. This hardly describes a man who was a cardsharp on trains—which in itself was not a likely possibility anyway, since railroad police and detectives would soon have started recognizing such repeat petty criminals and barring them from the trains. It has been suggested that Tom Morgan never even came along on the Coronado caper, because Kate had abandoned him and run away with a new lover. That seems in keeping with Kate's character. In any event, if John Longfield was having an affair with Kate, and we know he was telling his wife he was in Cleveland, there is every reason to think he would be on a train back to California. It is very likely that he and Kate were stringing poor Lizzie along, judging from Lizzie's actions. Longfield was probably bringing Lizzie's three trunks along (on his way to spend time with Kate Morgan) and had the claim checks in his pocket.

Lizzie somehow found out the love of her life was coming west. She took a train south to Anaheim, transferred to an east-west train to Orange or another station even further east. This would be the train John Longfield was on—and, coincidentally, Joseph A. Jones. The train was coming from Denver, where Jones must have had business, and John may have been traveling on this line from as far east as Cleveland or Hamburg, or both, having accomplished his business—sending his wife letters from General Delivery in Cleveland (she had no idea where her husband was staying), and setting up the credit for Lottie A. Bernard in Hamburg. Kate Morgan had the two men running around the country on errands, helping to set up her ruse, while she stayed close to Lizzie in Los Angeles. Kate was thus stringing John Longfield along, telling him she was going to fix his problem (getting rid of Lizzie), while she and he were both stringing Lizzie along (which reached its breaking point in the argument on the train, and no doubt precipitated Lizzie's growing doubts and her suicide a few days later).

Jones was to tell the bellman that he started becoming aware of a man and a woman—the woman he saw at the Hotel Del, Lottie A. Bernard (Lizzie)—having a heated discussion on the train as the train was approaching the (West) coast. This suggests he was not aware of them before that, and had no idea when she actually boarded the train. She might have done this during the evening of November 23, spent the night shivering in some train station a few hours east of Los Angeles, boarded the train he was on, gone from car to car, found him, and confronted him with a plea to divorce his wife and marry her, since he'd ruined her. Jones describes her tone as 'pleading.' This conjures a heart-rending and pathetic scenario. Jones says that her tone became more and more pleading, and then she repeatedly apologized to the man. The man, however, kept denying whatever she wanted, and finally stormed furiously off the train. Jones then took no further notice of her until he coincidentally spotted her in the lobby of the Hotel del Coronado later that day. The man—John Longfield—disappeared into the crowds with her baggage checks in his pocket, and Lizzie continued on her journey south to her final fate.

We can now roll the film forward to Day One.

Day 1—Thursday, Nov. 24, 1892 (Lottie Bernard Checks In)

It appears that Lottie A. Bernard ('A' as in Anderson, her aunt Louisa's name, and the name of the fictitious Mr. or Dr. M.C. Anderson) checked into the Hotel del Coronado in the afternoon of Thanksgiving Day. We don't know exactly what time she left Los Angeles the previous day, or when the episode on the train happened the next morning, but we know she made at least two stops in San Diego after leaving the train—and it would take several hours for her to reach the Hotel del Coronado, which is located at the far end of Coronado, across the bay from San Diego—so she couldn't have checked in at the Del much before mid-afternoon.

Lottie Bernard (Lizzie) got off the train at the old train station (long ago demolished) near today's Santa Fe Depot on Kettner Street and West Broadway (then D Street).

As her first stop, she went to the baggage depot nearby to claim her three trunks, but was refused because the tickets were (she said) in the pocket of her 'brother' and she had no idea where he was. The clerks refused to turn over the trunks to her without claim checks.

Junction 4th and C Streets, showing Hotel Brewster and Terminus of La Jolla Car Line.

Now she made her second stop. From the baggage depot, she walked several blocks up C Street to the corner of C Street and 4th Street (today's Fourth Avenue), where she spent a short amount of time (for mysterious reasons, to which I think I know the answer) at the Hotel Brewster. It was a novel idea of the 1890s—a hotel designed for businessmen (businesswomen were as yet a thought of the future), clean and efficient in every way. So why not just stay at the Brewster rather than go all the way to the most expensive resort in the area, the Hotel Del? She had little money, and no possessions but the clothes on her body and a little satchel or purse—so why would this doomed and beautiful young woman choose to bypass so many less pricey hotels and rooming houses? Why did she purposefully walk back down to the waterfront, take the ferry across to Coronado, and then take the trolley to the opposite end of the island to the Hotel del Coronado? Why pick the most expensive place in the area, and one located so far away? Because she was on a mission that must be accomplished at that very place, whose owner was the wealthy John Spreckels.

ℎ ∾

Why did Lizzie make the detour to the Hotel Brewster? According to eyewitnesses, she inquired there about her 'brother' and his wife, Mr. (Dr.?) and Mrs. Anderson. This fictitious doctor-brother was someone about whom she would repeatedly and anxiously keep asking the clerks at the Hotel Del in days to come.

I believe that there were two reasons for her going to the Hotel Brewster. One was to meet Kate Morgan, who would be hovering out of sight throughout this scenario. Kate Morgan would have already instructed her to refer to her lover as her 'brother,' as Kate was in the habit of referring to her husband and/or lover. It would add dignity and credibility if this 'brother' happened to be an accomplished man of stature and authority—a medical doctor. I believe Kate had lied to Lizzie, and Lizzie expected to meet Kate Morgan and either Tom Morgan or John Longfield at the Hotel Brewster.

The second reason for going to the Brewster was to pick up the medicines she would need to terminate her pregnancy. That much she surely received, perhaps from Kate Morgan directly, or from a desk clerk whom Kate had bribed a dollar to make a discreet handover.

In any case, somehow Kate Morgan had sent a message to Spreckels in San Francisco, telling him she was Charlotte Barnard (or some similar name, semi-disguised as Lottie Bernard) and he had gotten her pregnant. Now, to stay out of his hair, she needed a sum of money to take care of herself and her baby, or there would be trouble for Spreckels. The plan was for her to create a public spectacle to embarrass Spreckels before the world—and what better way than to have a messy, bloody, noisy, panic-inducing miscarriage right in the main lobby of Spreckels' hotel?

That in itself would solve nothing for Kate Morgan—would potentially kill Lizzie, and bring in no money—but the idea was that it wouldn't get to that. The idea was that Spreckels would quickly cave, and that Kate and John and Tom would remove Lizzie to the care of a doctor while they divided the money—how many ways is anyone's guess. Lizzie did not have the brains to think up such a complex scheme, however whacko it certainly was. Kate Morgan did possess the brains and the imagination, but it shows her ruthlessness and her detachment from reality and from human feelings. When Lizzie shot herself, it was out of very human, humane feelings—remorse, and a sense of betrayal. She had remorse not just for what she was doing ("I hardly know that man, I have only heard of him," she writes in a note found after hear death, most likely in reference to the man she was trying to harm, Spreckels). We can infer that she had been pregnant out of wedlock on a previous occasion, that she bore the baby, and that she was forced to give it up for adoption—a great hardship for many women today, but a social death sentence in Victorian times. We know that she was a handful for her mother, Elizabeth, and her loving sister, May. We know that she had to go into exile for a short while with her Aunt Louisa Anderson across the Michigan Panhandle in Grand Rapids, to escape her mother's wrath. We know that John Longfield's later letter to his wife refers to bad feelings between Lizzie and her mother. All of this is to say that, as she neared her suicide, Lizzie felt terrible not only about the blackmail scheme against a man she did not know, who had done her no harm; but also about having disappointed her mother and sister again by getting pregnant with a married man in an openly and irresponsibly flaunted relationship that got Lizzie, John, and sister May all fired from Bin & Hammond; and no doubt about the fact that she was killing (destroying, if you will) her unborn child. Whatever views one takes on abortion, if we put ourselves in the head of this beautiful, and in some ways childlike, woman, we can well suppose that she felt the unborn child was being subjected to the same horrific pain that was beginning to seize Lizzie herself ("she was groaning," one witness said of her. "She appeared to be suffering intensely," said Harry West). The pain of an extramarital pregnancy was nothing new to Lizzie—and something she could not bear to endure again. Nor would Victorian society forgive her. Without marriage to John Longfield, she was a ruined woman, and might as well dramatically throw herself off a cliff. Or shoot herself, as she did.

Lizzie, who arrived in sparkling good health on Thursday, started taking these medicines and her condition rapidly deteriorated until, within a day or two, she could hardly walk or stand by Monday. Dr. Mertzman testified to this effect at the Coroner's Inquest, adding that he was sure she was pregnant, had borne a child before, and that she was taking 'terrible medicines' to induce a miscarriage. Let's examine the ominous signs of what Lizzie was doing (on Kate's instructions).

Among the artifacts found in the dead woman's hotel room was a bottle of pills (most likely laudanum) with instructions "If this does not relieve you, you better send for the doctor" (signed, 'Druggist')."[60]

❧ ❧

From the Hotel Brewster, she makes her way back down to the harbor, across the bay, and across Coronado to the Hotel del Coronado. There, she has the clerk sign her in. At some point, the man who signs in after her (Joseph Jones) recognizes her as the woman he saw arguing and pleading with the angry man on the train near Orange and Anaheim. Then she goes upstairs to Room 302, where she locks the door and prepares to start taking her medicines.

❧ ❧

An interesting question occurs in regard to this scenario. If it is a blackmail plot, and Spreckels is now aware of the threat, we must assume that the Spreckels Machine is in high gear. Spreckels is busy in Washington, so he has people locally hard at work (the Spreckels Machine, my term for the shadowy underside of the official Spreckels Company), blunting this situation as best they can. Now normally, even today, if an attractive young woman arrives to check in out of a clear blue sky at a hotel, traveling alone and without luggage, it is natural for a hotel clerk to at least momentarily think of prostitution if there is something somehow odd or salacious about her behavior on top of the rest. It isn't the first thought, but it hovers in the periphery. If you work at a hotel, there is always a certain small amount of illegal traffic that managers do their best to root out, and which doormen and valets (and shuttle drivers) talk about.

When Elisha Babcock laid out the master plan for Coronado, he stipulated it would be a dry city—with one exception, the bar at the Hotel Del. Coronado was to be a health resort, and this was the time of Kellogg's corn flakes and health nuts and the temperance movement. Also, he most certainly did not wish for his town to become another Stingaree, like the venue across the Bay, from which one could hear distant gunshots, laughter, and screams by day or night.

It seems remarkable that Lottie A. Bernard was allowed to sign in at all—in an era when it was frowned upon for a woman to travel alone.[61] Now this is just gratuitous speculation, but it occurs to me that, maybe, the chief clerk (A.S. Gomer) was tipped off to let her register. What better location to have her, than directly under Spreckels' roof, for his detectives to observe if she was really acting alone (an aggrieved, desperate girl) or if she was a crook aided by accomplices?

Day 2—Friday, Nov. 25, 1892

She starts asking Chief Clerk A.S. Gomer if her 'brother' has left any messages, and mentions the problem about the claim checks and her three trunks—which are still stuck at the baggage depot, and will remain there until they disappear. She tells Gomer that she is expecting her 'brother,' 'Dr. Anderson,' to arrive at any time to take care of her because she is ill. She claims to be suffering from a vague and over-diagnosed contemporary ailment called 'neuralgia' (Gr. *Neuron,* 'tendon, nerve' + *algesis,* 'pain'). There is a more specific modern ailment with this name—an inflamed nerve or tendon—but in Lizzie's time, the word covered a host of psychological and psychosomatic as well as physiological illnesses. The only known cure was to send you to the seashore, so nobody was surprised that a young woman suffering from neuralgia would show up to recuperate at the Hotel Del.

❧ ❧

Day 3—Saturday, Nov. 26, 1892

On the third day at the Hotel del Coronado, real estate agent T. J. Fisher says she came into the hotel drugstore, where he shared an office with the druggist. Fisher says she wandered about 'slowly' and apparently 'in pain.' She asked for medicine to ease her pain (described as 'intense suffering'). Fosdick suggested she consult a doctor, and she told him that her brother, a physician, would be arriving any day. The elusive 'Dr. Anderson' would never show up nor send word. We can be sure the only man she felt so strongly about was John Longfield.

Later in the day, Harry West would rather vaguely remember, she asked him to get her an empty pint bottle and a sponge from the hotel drugstore. This request seems innocent and enigmatic until one really considers what it was about—something I had not yet considered while writing the first edition of this book.

One ancient method of inducing an abortion or a miscarriage was to insert a medically treated sponge, called a pessary, into the vaginal canal as close to the womb as possible. Pessaries, from the Greek *pessos,* 'pebble' or 'stone,' could be used for various other local applications—for example, as a suppository. This procedure for aborting was known as far back as in ancient Egypt. The empty bottle she requested would be for mixing and storing her medicine for repeated applications. She used the sponge as a pessary. The occasional requests for wine or whiskey were as palliatives to ease her pain and discomfort, along with the laudanum she was taking. Bit by bit, as we interpret the minute little known facts that have come down to us, the story begins to swim into focus like a photograph in a fixative bath. What we should carry away from this is a sense of horror at the suffering of this poor, lovely, befuddled woman—and the heartlessness of the people around her, except kind and compliant Harry West and an unnamed housekeeping woman who occasionally helped her.[62]

Day 4—Sunday, Nov. 27, 1892

No activity known. We can surmise that she ate little, and spent most of the time in her room feeling sicker and sicker. She had time to reflect, also, that she was being betrayed. Nevertheless, we know that as shortly before her death as Monday evening she still asked about the elusive Dr. Anderson one last time. But think about this. Compare her behavior on Saturday, when she started the pessary, with her behavior on Monday, when she had difficulty walking. And on Monday, she would already be drinking alcohol in the morning—to ease her acute pain. It is possible we know nothing of her activities Sunday because she may have been in bed, semi-conscious, as her 'terrible medicines' (as Dr. Mertzman called them) started to take hold of her and ravage her—even as it became clear she had been betrayed and abandoned, and had little room for hope. We can only imagine her suffering that day, alone in her room.

Day 5—Monday, Nov. 28, 1892

In the morning on the fifth day, Lottie had Harry West bring her a glass of wine from the bar, and later a whiskey cocktail. She had him bring a pitcher of ice water—she drank these alcoholic beverages early in the day—to dull her pain, we can be sure.

Around noon, she had Harry West dry her hair after she'd fallen in the bath. He would later testify that he found her suffering and groaning a great deal, and sleeping much of the day. He would tell investigators that she seemed to sleep a while, wake up, spend time groaning in pain, and then fall back to sleep. He said she again mentioned her brother, Dr. Anderson, who would soon join her.

Between noon and 1:00 p.m., Harry West and Gomer went to visit her in Room 302 to inquire about her health. Gomer grilled her about her finances. She told Gomer she had stomach cancer, obviously a fib. She also assured him that credit would be available to cover her expense tab. She suggested he telegraph a G. L. Allen in Hamburg, Iowa (Kate Morgan's home town) for the needed funds—and a credit for $25 arrived from a Hamburg bank on Tuesday morning, just after Lottie or Lizzie was found dead.

A great sea storm was approaching, making her room gloomy and cold. She had thus far refused to light the fireplace. Perhaps she was burning up with fever, as the expression goes. During the afternoon, Harry West gave her a few matches, and she began to burn a stack of papers (possibly including letters) in the fireplace. Neither Gomer nor Harry got a good look at what these papers might be.

That afternoon, Lottie went downstairs to the pharmacy. Real estate agent T. J Fisher described her as walking very slowly, and appearing to be in great pain. During their conversation, she indicated she planned to go across the Bay to San Diego, and he warned her against doing so, because of her condition, and the coming storm. Lottie replied that she had to go, and then made a statement that appears somewhat unfocused and out of kilter with already established facts (or fibs).[63] From what Fisher quoted at the Coroner's Inquest, she said that she must make the trip. She said that she forgot her baggage claim [tickets], and that she must go over (the Bay) "to identify my trunks, personally." Earlier, she said she knew where the tickets (checks) were—her brother had taken them when they were separated at Orange the past Thursday. The clerks refused to hand the trunks over on that day, and there is no reason to think that anything had changed since then. It is more likely that Lottie had at least one very different reason [to buy a gun], maybe two [to see someone, like maybe Kate Morgan, conjecturally staying at the Hotel Brewster?], to make what must be an extremely painful and difficult journey, and that she concocted this story to throw him off the trail. There are lots of little bits of evidence like this that Lottie liked to fib, like a somewhat air-headed young girl, and her fibs tended to be somewhat clumsy, like when she told Gomer she was dying of stomach cancer,[64] blurting that out to get rid of him.

Between 4:00 and 5:00 p.m. (there is confusion about whether she was in San Diego as early as 3:00 p.m., or later) Lottie journeyed to downtown San Diego. Crossing the bay, she went to Fifth Avenue and bought a gun and cartridges, as mentioned in Part III.

There is a time, after she left the last known store, when her movements are unaccounted for. Could she have gone back to the Hotel Brewster to seek out Kate Morgan one last time and tell her the show was off, she wanted out, and where was John Longfield? Chances are Kate Morgan understood by then that Spreckels' agents were not about to pay her off, and that she and Longfield had already skipped town.

Lizzie on the other hand, wracked with pain and guilt, may have considered killing Kate Morgan and John Longfield. We'll never know. She made the painful journey back to Coronado because that's where her only possessions were—in that handbag—and because she had no recourse left but to return to where her fate would play out its final act.

At 6:30 p.m., bellman Harry West says he saw Lottie on a hotel veranda overlooking the ocean. It was dark by then, and there was an air of dread and excitement as the atmospheric monster approached. It was the last time Harry would see Lottie alive.

Lottie made one more stop at the front desk to ask Gomer if there was any word from Dr. Anderson. That was between 7:00 and 8:00 p.m., and she was told there had not yet been any word from her 'brother.' This was the last time anyone saw her alive.

People stood on balconies around the Hotel, looking southwest over the Pacific Ocean. They watched in awe as the black clouds of the storm rolled closer, and raged and thundered. Some guests may have requested relocation to the landward side of the Hotel. Nobody heard a gunshot fired, during the night, on the beach just behind the hotel.

Day 6—Tuesday, Nov. 29, 1892 (Body Found)

Electrician David Cone found Lottie's body at 8:20 a.m.. Cone found (my words) a mannequin-like body lying on the concrete steps overlooking the beach, which was not far from the sea in those days. When he realized it was a woman's dead body, he saw that her clothing was all wet, and "the body seemed to have been lying there quite a while; to have been dead quite a while."[65]

℞ ℟

There is a fine detail here that calls for some remedial conjecture. The next day, at the Coroner's Inquest, witnesses say that there was blood on the steps, along with the large gun. The question is: how could there be blood on the steps when the area, and the body, had been inundated by a violent rain and possibly the thundering surf during the night's storm?

This is an important question because there has circulated some urban lore that she was murdered or that something else happened rather than a straightforward suicide—a hypothesis discounted by official sources, and I concur. A more complex interpretation requires yet more conjecture, so I prefer to navigate the simplest course among the many baffling clues. If she had died in the morning, after the storm, does that somehow open the door to other possibilities? Who knows. Because there was blood on the steps, does this mean that she died after the rain storm? We don't know what time the worst of the rain ended, but we can surmise that, even if the downpour ended between 2:00 and 3:00 a.m. (which Stetson pegged as the time of death), there would have been drizzle for a time. The blood would have been watery, and one finds it hard to imagine this not being mentioned; but then the coroner's inquest does not mention the copious black powder residue that suicide would have left on her hand and face—did the rain wash this away, or was she shot by another person from a distance, with a slightly different-caliber handgun? I don't know. I can only show it is possible she did kill herself during the storm.

Regarding powder residue, it is possible that might have washed away in a severe downpour—which would also have washed any blood away; so how could there be blood on the steps? It's possible that, when she shot herself, she fell backward in something like a sitting position (as Cone attested). The gun had a trigger guard, and would have stayed on her hand until she lay still, and it dropped down a step from her finger. From the impact and entry wound on her right temple, her head was turned slightly to the left, tilted to one side. That meant some amount of blood could not escape from the entry wound (there was no exit wound). Blood clots formed in the entry wound. When Cone found her, he may have slapped her face in a hysterical and unthinking attempt to revive her. The majority of people are right-handed, so that probably makes sense. A right-handed slap to the left cheek might have turned her head to the right (despite rigor mortis). Cone, as we know, ran off as fast as he could to get Gomer, but returned with the gardener for another look, and then the two men were caught up in such a dither that each ran a different way around the hotel to get Gomer. One or more slaps would loosen any blood clots in the entry wound. Cone left, came back with Koeppen, and they both ran off again. Meanwhile, residual blood and fluids could have leaked from the open skull, down the arm, puddling under her finger and around the gun. There was said to be blood 'under' the gun, but that could just as well mean 'around' the gun. This suggests that there no problem between the fact that blood was found, and the fact that there was a rain storm. In other words, I do not see this as ruling out suicide during the storm. While I do not rule out the murder hypothesis, I feel that hypothesis requires a lot more conjectural stretches, and the suicide hypothesis is entirely reasonable.

જી ભ

What about the credit from Hamburg, Iowa? It seems likely, for whatever reason—maybe as simple as the fact that she knew the place, or it was convenient for some other reason, like there was a trusted accomplice—Kate Morgan chose that place to establish a credit alibi or cover, that she sent John Longfield to deliver $25 to the bank manager, and explain it was to be sent if someone from California asked for it on behalf of an old school friend's wife. It would have been impossible for anyone from that area (Kate or Tom Morgan) to pull this off, because everyone would have recognized them. It could have been done by telegram, but the bank officer specifically said a man came to see him.

A conjectural scenario to cover all this is that (a) Kate Morgan sent John Longfield to set up the credit scenario for use later, as transpired; (b) John Longfield traveled on to Cleveland to set up a General Delivery address at the main post office to cover his tracks with his wife—note that Cleveland is part of a cluster of cities around Lake Ontario that become important in the story, and it's not far from Hamburg; (c) Kate Morgan and John Longfield had become an item, unbeknownst to Lizzie or probably to Tom, if the latter was still on the scene, and this would motivate John to make the trip back to California to see Kate—as well as deliver Lizzie's three trunks from wherever they had been stashed, and possibly to lie to Lizzie—although he then told Lizzie on the train that he didn't intend to divorce his wife. What he probably told Lizzie was that he would think about it, and that she should think about how rich they were all going to be (after blackmailing Spreckels) and how her pregnancy problem was about to be solved. When Lizzie pressed him, he became angry, and she apologized, but he stormed off the train, forgetting to give her the baggage claim checks. She rode on to San Diego, and tried to redeem the trunks at the baggage terminal. It is not clear whether the baggage claim scene happened before or after her walk to the Hotel Brewster. It would have taken a little time, after the train arrived, to unload the baggage car and wheel loads of suitcases and trunks to the baggage depot.

I do think Lizzie remained convinced he would come to help her at the Hotel Del, under the guise of being her 'brother,' the doctor, for whom she kept anxiously asking at the desk. When she kept pressing him to divorce his wife, he grew angry and stormed off the train, never to see her again.

I mentioned above that it is possible that Tom Morgan and Kate had separated already. The reason we suspect there was yet another man involved is because the testimony from the bank manager in Hamburg, Iowa, suggests there were two men who set up the credit scheme. It is possible that Kate (who was alone when she visited her uncle in Hanford) was at that point alone, and that she somehow encountered John and Lizzie in Detroit and enmeshed them in her scheme. The second man, little more than a phantom, might have been an old friend of Kate's in Hamburg. There is also mention of a 'professional gambler' being in the Hamburg area—but this could be anybody. It is sometimes assumed this was Tom, but there is nothing conclusive.

❧ ❧

Sometime between 9:30 and 10:00 a.m., on Tuesday, Nov. 29, after the body had been found, Deputy Coroner H. J. Stetson arrived from the mainland with a crew to remove the body. Given the critical juncture a few days hence, when the identification changed from Lizzie Wyllie to Kate Morgan, we wonder how the body was handled, and what changes might have occurred before and after embalming.

Stetson estimated Lottie had been dead about six or seven hours, meaning she shot herself (or was murdered, by some persistent rumors) between 2:00 and 3:00 a.m. That would mean that from about (splitting the difference) 2:30 a.m. to 7:30 a.m., the body lay on the steps for five hours while the storm abated. From the time of discovery to the time Stetson and his crew arrived, about two hours passed—remarkable in that they had to be summoned. There was rudimentary, early telephone service to the mainland from the hotel itself, and there was always the telegraph. Stetson would then gather his men, walk or ride several blocks from the police headquarters on Fifth Street to the waterfront, and then ride the ferry ("the next boat")[66] across to Coronado. The crossing would take 15 minutes on the steam-powered ferry, or up to 30 minutes rowing, or sailing and tacking, depending on the winds; and we can presume the Bay was still a little rough, in the aftermath of the storm. Stetson and his men would then cross the island, a distance of 1.3 miles to the Hotel del Coronado from the ferry landing, which can be walked in a leisurely twenty to thirty minutes. Stetson's crew took the body to Johnson & Company Mortuary at 907 Sixth Street.

Given the high mortality rate in the Stingaree, in addition to normal coverage for a city of then 16,000 souls, it is likely that a coroner's crew could easily be assembled on short notice—in fact, this segues into a parallel question: how did the Coroner managed to assemble nine jurors for the inquest the next day? And yet another question—if there was a formal inquest, literally a jury trial, why was there no autopsy?

Two hours from the time of notification to the time of removal is a remarkable efficiency, which in itself raises some questions. It makes one wonder if it was an anticipated event. This is not the same as suggesting she may have been murdered. It is quite likely, in the blackmail scenario, the Spreckels Machine had numerous operatives attentively monitoring events surrounding the Beautiful Stranger.

How much did the body deteriorate before it was embalmed at least half a day after her death? We don't know if it was packed in ice, but we can be sure it was embalmed, because she lay in state. The matter of the pierced ears will come up in the days to follow, as the I.D. shifts from Lottie Bernard to Katie Logan to Lizzie Wyllie, and finally to Kate Morgan. This final change was made on the basis of a flimsy matter—the body did not have pierced ears, and neither did Kate Morgan, but Lizzie did. I don't feel this discrepancy is enough to shift the I.D. away from Lizzie. First of all, her mother said she was broke after being fired from her job. She and Longfield had no money. Would she not have pawned her silver earrings? If she had her ears pierced recently, it is possible that the holes would have closed up. If the body lay exposed for hours, and then was packed in sawdust or canvas without benefit of ice, and then embalmed at Johnson Company, what physical deterioration can we expect, particularly in peripheral soft tissue like the ear lobes? Far more important to the identification would be the two small moles on the left cheek, which both the corpse and Lizzie Wyllie had—and Lizzie's mother was bereaved and convinced the dead woman was her daughter.

Day 7—Wednesday Nov. 30, 1892 (Coroner's Inquest)

The next morning, before the Coroner's Inquest, the leading physician and surgeon in town, Dr. B. F. Mertzman, did a half-hour examination of the body. He was not permitted to autopsy her, but he would testify briefly at the inquest. He is undoubtedly the medical authority later quoted off-record in the newspapers as saying she did not have stomach cancer but most likely shot herself "over some love affair." That same medical authority said he felt she had borne a child before, was now pregnant, and was taking 'terrible medicines' to induce a miscarriage.

ॐ ॐ

In recent times, much has been made of an alleged discrepancy between the caliber of the gun and the caliber of the bullet. Dr. B. F. Mertzman estimates the caliber to be "about .38 or .40." There was no exit wound. The bullet stayed in the brain, despite the considerable caliber of the cartridge, and murder proponents have suggested that a second person (possibly Tom Morgan or, following my presentation, agents of the Spreckels Machine) used a smaller caliber gun, maybe a .38, with a lesser charge of gunpowder. Such arguments are not persuasive at all, in my opinion.

An expert on guns (Mr. Richard Agler; see "Acknowledgement" at front of this volume) told me the gun would have used black powder, and the charge was probably weakened by dampness in the rain. In fact, remembering the discussion of blood on the steps, this expert said (and I have since confirmed by further research) that people who commit suicide by shooting themselves using black powder propellants always have a thick coating of oily black residue in two places—on the shooting hand, and around the entry wound. That means the dead woman should have had significant traces of black powder residue all over her right hand and all over the right side of her head. Strangely, there is no mention of this—

which suggests the residue was washed away by rain, and that in turn tends to confirm that she died before the storm ended—which leaves us with the slapping hypothesis to explain the blood on the steps.

Chick testifies he recognizes the gun he sold her by the rust on it, which supports information on the Internet that this particular weapon was essentially a throwaway or a 'suicide special.' This gun was not a brand name or a model, but a generic ('American Bulldog') which itself was a variant on a generic ('Bulldog') copied from a copy of a standard 1887 British Army revolver, the .455 caliber Webley Mark II. First, this army weapon was made commercially available in the United Kingdom as the British Bulldog. A variant across the Channel was called the Belgian Bulldog. The U.S. variant was produced by a number of manufacturers, with a number of calibers, under the name American Bulldog. Compared to most handguns, it was a relatively dainty piece at the standard .32 caliber. The gun sold to Lottie Bernard was a .45 variant, with a grotesquely enlarged and re-engineered five-bullet cylinder that made it seem larger than it was, because the grip and the barrel maintained the same relative smallness as on the .32. Suffice it to say, when the bystander said "She is going to hurt herself with that gun," most likely he echoed the sort of comments usually made in regard to cheap Saturday Night Specials. He was not commenting on her mannerisms, but on the rusty and untrustworthy weapon Chick sold her.

વ્ઝ ન્જ

Stetson testifies that, while examining her room, he found a valise. He also found an envelope she had addressed to *Denman Thompson, The Old Homestead*. This refers to one of the most famous actors of the day, Denman Thompson of New Hampshire. According to a contemporary critic, "Thompson interpreted America to itself in the core persona of the solid New England farmer." Thompson's play is, essentially, about a New England rustic who journeys to a big city, is the victim of many misadventures, and returns happily to the simple and honest country life. It seems Lizzie had seen the great thespian's play, and wanted to write a fan letter while she was sitting in her lonely room at the Hotel Del, waiting for the medicine to wreak its painful changes, and still hoping for a signal from 'Dr. M.C. Anderson' (Kate? John?) that Spreckels had paid, and that she could get out.

There is another theater reference of interest. It seems the poor, benighted girl left behind an invitation by Louise Leslie Carter and Lillian Russell to the Hotel del Coronado. Carter and Russell were two of the most famous stage actresses of the day. Like all the items surrounding the late Mr. Bernard, each of these items elicits stunned and silent puzzlement in the courtroom. Was the girl hallucinating? Did she concoct fantasies about being asked to this great hotel by two famous actresses? She whiled her time away in fantasies like this, composing dreamy letters from great actresses who, in her imagination, invited her to this famous resort.

છૂ ન્ડ

Stetson found a piece of paper on which was written the word Frank four times: *Frank Frank Frank Frank*. Who knows what to make of that? In Chapter 10 of my novel Lethal Journey, I playfully make this a reference to a frequent later visitor to the Hotel Del, none other than L. Frank Baum, the author of *The Wizard of Oz*. While that book was not published until 1900, it is known that Baum came to San Diego and presumably Coronado during the 1890s to scout out health resort possibilities, and the Theosophical Society at Point Loma. I do not positively suggest this was the Frank of whom she wrote. Maybe she'd had an old boyfriend named Frank in Detroit. Maybe he was the first lout who got her pregnant and helped her lose her innocence—clearly, she was terribly traumatized and alone in the growing fog of pain, drugs, fear, remorse, and despair. Whoever Frank was, she obviously wished he were there to comfort her.

છૂ ન્ડ

Stetson found another scrap of paper on which she had written: "I merely heard of that man. I do not know him." I take this to be a clear reference to the owner of the Hotel del Coronado, John Spreckels, whose reputation she was helping Kate Morgan besmirch. It sounds like the beginning of a written confession. It sounds as if she is full of remorse at being the vehicle to accuse a man she had never met of making her pregnant. Unlike Kate Morgan—who seems sociopathically incapable of doubt or remorse, and John Longfield not much better ('a rounder,' as the newspapers cited his low reputation around Detroit[67])—Lizzie is really the only actor in this drama with real, human feelings. That makes her situation all the more tragic and pathetic.

છૂ ન્ડ

Stetson mentions another innocent little detail that is yet one more piece of critical evidence. In the room were several embroidered hankies. Some of them clearly had the name Louisa Anderson on them—which was the name of Lizzie Wyllie's aunt in Grand Rapids, where Lizzie fled after her mother discovered Lizzie was once again pregnant out of wedlock, this time by the married John Longfield.

Remarkably, a similar set of hankies, with 'Louisa Anderson' embroidered on them, will shortly appear in a trunk owned by Kate

Morgan, at the L.A. Grants' house in Los Angeles, where the pseudonymous Katie Logan worked. More than anything (except Katie Logan blurting out that her name was really Lizzie), the objects in that Los Angeles trunk tie the two women together—we'll get to that shortly.

Somehow, at the Coroner's Inquest, the detail of the hankies got lost in the shuffle, despite the fact that the middle name used by the fictitious Lottie A. Bernard was 'Anderson.'

More stunning is the fact that Stetson stumbles over a name on some faded hankies, clearly embroidered with the last name Anderson; but but he says he can't read the first name—which he says looks like 'Little,' but is almost certainly name Lizzie.

The find of these hankies is one of the most important in the entire case. The hankies in the hotel room point to Lottie Bernard being Lizzie Wyllie. The hankies in Los Angeles tie Kate Morgan and Lizzie Wyllie together. Kate was training Lizzie to be an impersonator, under the name Katie Logan. Kate parked her trunk with Lizzie, because Kate was busy traveling around setting up the caper in Coronado. As part of her manipulation, she had to keep dangling the carrot of John Longfield before Lizzie, which is why the poor girl was running around in Los Angeles during her off-hours, presumably trying to get some sort of papers put together pertaining to the divorce she wanted John to get so he could marry her. She may have confronted Longfield on the train with those very papers—first rather pushy about it, which made him angry, and then pleading and apologetic as she began to realize it would not be so easy for him. Lizzie undoubtedly had a set of her own hankies (and it is possible they were her mother's since they were so faded; maybe 'Little' or 'Lizzie' was actually Elizabeth, the mother, who had a set in common with her sister, Louisa; and Louisa gave poor Lizzie some of her own hankies to cry into while Lizzie was staying with her in Grand Rapids).

ès ÷

Under further questioning, Stetson says that he examined the grate in the room, and found some papers that had burned entirely to ashes. A nightgown hung on a hook. On the mantel were a hat, a bottle, and a penknife. One wonders if that was the bottle she used to imbue her pessary. And where had the sponge gone? Had she finished her doses (the bottle was empty) and thrown the sponge away? Was it still inside her? It was a common contraceptive device, so the doctor might not have mentioned it in court out of Victorian modesty. If the undertakers found it, they might not have thought much of it for the same reason.

Among the other bottles in the room were one with camphor (a topical anesthetic) and alcohol—a considerably quantity of brandy. Lizzie was most likely somewhat inebriated on Sunday as the medicine clawed her in its grip. There were some quinine pills, and a bottle of some kind that had a notice wrapped around it: "If it does not relieve you, you better send for the doctor." The notice was signed "Druggist," without a name or address. This type of medicine was not something you bought in a pharmacy without a prescription and a lot of questions, so this could be one reason for Lizzie's side trip to the Hotel Brewster upon her arrival. And the 'druggist' was probably not a licensed practitioner, but a quack of the same variety who performed back-alley abortions.

ℂ ℂ

The coroner states that the court has received all the testimony it can get, and asks the jury to issue its finding. It is afternoon, and the entire proceeding has taken less than one day. Why was Dr. Mertzman not permitted to do an autopsy? Why were some potentially important witnesses, like Joseph A. Jones of Boston, not subpoenaed? It is not clear that Jones' comment had been passed along to the press by this time. The haste of the proceeding—selecting nine jurors, albeit probably from a ready roll—and the brevity of the inquest suggest that the city, which was heavily in thrall to Spreckels, was in a hurry to get things over with.

It is remarkable that the woman's real identity had not been established by the end of the day and this hasty trial. Granted, they thought she really was Mrs. Lottie A. Bernard, whose husband or whose doctor brother were expected to soon inquire after her. Still, without knowing anything about her, it is difficult to see that they could firmly discount murder and opt for suicide, when there was no clear motive.

And then, the official transcript of the inquest is 'lost' for some time, and then restored with a handwritten note by a city clerk to the effect that it was misplaced.[68] By modern standards, the chain of property on the document was thus lost, and it could potentially have been tampered with. It has been suggested that perhaps the official transcript was 'held up' until her identity could be firmly established, but government entities do not 'misplace' an official transcript for such reasons.

Finally, also, the way the I.D. of the body would soon change several times on the flimsiest of grounds, ultimately to a woman (Kate Morgan) whose character was questionable, makes one wonder if there was not some manipulation going on by the Spreckels Machine to cast aspersion on the character of the (we presume) blackmailers (Tom and Kate Morgan) in a further effort to inoculate John Spreckels' good name. The County issued a death certificate, naming her as 'Lottie A. Bernard, a.k.a. Kate Morgan,' and—remarkably—gave the wrong date for her death. The given date is Monday, November 28, when the Coroner stated she died in the early hours of Tuesday, November 29. If they misplaced the transcript and then found it again, and if they got the date of death wrong, then what other blunders (or cover-ups) are there in this case?

Newspaper Accounts Dec. 1-Dec. 14

Day 8—Thursday, Dec. 1, 1892

Newspapers are beginning to wonder if there was something more to the relationship between Lottie Bernard and her purported 'brother.' If he were truly her brother, the reasoning went, he would have contacted authorities. News of her suicide was telegraphed all over the country, avidly followed by the Yellow Press. Speculation was immediately rife (couched in Victorian circumlocution) that the mysterious 'brother' was her lover—the man who ruined, betrayed, and abandoned her. This scent of scandal is known to have promoted the story to overnight national sensation in the Yellow Press. Press reports also speculated that her lover was 'highly placed.'

A leading medical authority (presumably Dr. B. F. Mertzman) affirms that she seemed healthy, and he dismisses as 'nonsense' the idea that she was so near death from cancer that doctors had pronounced her case hopeless. Mertzman states "The indications are that she has already borne a child, and was [pregnant] when she died, but this cannot be definitely proven without a post-mortem examination."[69] In the official haste to close the case, in a city effectively owned by John Spreckels, and lacking much of a police department, there was inordinate haste to get the coroner's inquest over and done. The doctor opines that she shot herself over "some love affair." He references her three-hour horseback ride with Charles Stevens on her first day at the Hotel del Coronado. Young Charlie said the woman was in good spirits, but seemed troubled.

Now we see the first mention that Lottie stopped at the Hotel Brewster after arriving in San Diego but before venturing to Coronado and signing in at the Hotel del Coronado. At the Brewster, Lottie asked about the arrival of her presumable brother and his wife, Mr. and Mrs. Anderson." Nobody by that name had signed in at the Brewster. Interestingly, she apparently did not refer to her 'brother' as Dr. Anderson, if this account is correct, but as Mr. Anderson.

అం⇆ఆ

Newspaper stories are beginning to question her identity, citing 'contradictory stories told by the victim' and the many contradictions and inconsistencies of the entire episode.

Day 9—Friday, Dec. 2, 1892

Newspapers speculate with increasing fervor that "the beautiful and mysterious stranger" killed herself over "love-trouble." A bellman reports the comments of Joseph E. (or A.) Jones regarding the argument on the train. The papers report that people feel her trip to San Diego was 'an escapade,' because she arrived without baggage. [Those people may not have been aware of the three trunks she said were being kept for her at the baggage office of the train terminal.] People noted the familiarity with which she spoke of Los Angeles hotels, which made it sound as if she had traveled much.

Employees at the Hotel del Coronado made comments indicating that the woman had been well-dressed and elegant, unlike the unattractive features associated with Kate Morgan from the photos that would soon be found in Kate's trunk in Los Angeles.

As the days are going by, doubts and loose ends proliferate. I believe it is logical to assume that the Spreckels Machine was not passive. Logically, having deflected the main element of the threat, now that Lottie was dead and her companions had disappeared, the Spreckels Machine continued manipulating behind the scenes. Remember, these people were nation-builders. They had, in effect, taken over the sovereign nation of Hawai'i by manipulating its royal cabinet, and now they were at war with a rival corporate gang set upon toppling them and their monarch, and putting Dole's faction in charge of the nation. Although the Spreckels family were shaken, and were about to lose Hawai'i, they still had vast resources and political power. Claus Spreckels, even as he was conducting shuttle diplomacy in Honolulu, and had his son John lobbying the President and Congress in Washington, was already plotting an alternative course, just in case. Spreckels had been experimenting in California with sugar beets since the 1870s. Now he easily switched sugar production to the area around Monterey, California, in the Salinas Valley.[70] Instead of sugar cane, his raw material became sugar beets. He would be fully operational by 1899, and the tiny town of Spreckels would be named after him. Immediately, his factory would be the world's largest refiner of sugar beets. These were people who had enormous resources, tens of thousands of employees in many places, and a vested interest in preventing John Spreckels' name from being besmirched by petty crooks at this critical time. For these reasons, I think it is reasonable to look for the unseen and dark hand of the Spreckels Machine in *l'affaire Lottie*.

Day 10—Saturday, Dec. 3, 1892

The identity shifts toward Lizzie, while the Hamburg, Iowa, bank and G. L. Allen come into play. Police confirm there are three trunks at the D Street baggage depot, which had shipped from Omaha, via Denver— Denver being, we recall, the point of departure of James Jones, who told a bellman he had seen Lottie in an argument with a well-dressed man on that train. The trunks could not be opened without authorization from higher-ups in the baggage hierarchy.

Take note, again, that the Spreckels Company controlled much of Greater San Diego, including Coronado. There were actually two companies in San Diego with the Spreckels name, one run by John Spreckels, the other owned by John's brother Adolph, who would gain notoriety as a young man of 27, when in 1884, in public view, he shot the publisher of The San Francisco Chronicle over an editorial critical of Claus Spreckels. The publisher, Michael de Young, lived, and Spreckels was acquitted after pleading insanity. Adolph would die in 1924 from pneumonia, after being weakened by decades of syphilis. His flamboyant wife, Alma, was famous for both her philanthropies and her extravagant lifestyle.[71] Spreckels is a sacred name in both San Francisco and San Diego, but the reality is that they were a family of real people, endowed with greatness on one hand, and equally grandiose foible on the other hand. So it is not a leap of imagination to suppose that there was a dark side to it all. The fact that John Spreckels owned the major newspapers in San Diego, and lavished the city with endowments, ensured that his legacy would be a bright one. In this book, we want to dispassionately look at the nimbus of mystery surrounding the Lottie A. Bernard affair, and try to make sense of the muddle—including a recognition that John Spreckels had a vested interest in covering his good name. The fact that Lottie Bernard was allowed to check into the Hotel Del in the first place, despite her traveling alone and without baggage, showing up as a dusty and attractive young woman without visible means, could have aroused enough suspicion to call for a check of her means and connections, and a refusal to allow her to check in. The haste with which the Coroner's men arrived, and the haste of the jury trial the next day, and its inconclusive result, suggest that the Spreckels Machine that virtually ran the city wanted this affair put behind. The 'loss' and 'rediscovery' of the official transcript of the jury trial opens the possibility that the permanent record was tampered with by the Spreckels Machine. It would probably have been enough to let it go there. However, just in case the blackmail story did leak, it was an effective touch to make the dead woman be Kate Morgan. She was essentially an unsavory person, who was now cast in the Yellow Press (with input from the Spreckels Machine, funded by the Spreckels fortune) as a grifter and a gambler's wife. There is no doubt that the Yellow Press had a lurid momentum all its own, but it is quite possible that the Spreckels Machine seeded the kernels of various scandalous threads to obfuscate the issue as well as set up a pair of villains at the heart of the story. As the record tells us, sources both anonymous and named (e.g., Swarts) popped up out of nowhere and chimed in with distracting leads that create ambiguities. As it turned out, the underlying story was effectively squelched, and the result is the tantalizing and salacious mystery story we are endeavoring to finally resolve today, in this book, after more than a century of mythology and a world-class ghost story.

Day 11—Sunday, Dec. 4, 1892

The San Diego Union identifies the dead woman as Lizzie Wyllie of Detroit, and we learn that Lizzie and May had worked for Binn & Hammond in Detroit, where Lizzie had an affair with her foreman, and both sisters and John Longfield had been fired.

The Los Angeles Herald reports[72] that Mrs. Elizabeth Wyllie of Detroit positively identified the body as her daughter's, based on pictures and descriptions sent to her from San Diego. Among the effects were jewelry, which arouses our curiosity. Elizabeth Wyllie stated Longfield and her daughter were broke when they fled Detroit. I have guessed that Lizzie may have sold her silver earrings. It is possible that Kate Morgan bribed Lizzie with jewelry and clothes, but that is pure speculation. However, Mrs. Wyllie provides us with a substantial timeline for her daughter's activities. We know she went to stay with her Aunt Louisa, whose hankies showed up in Kate Morgan's trunk in Los Angeles. The reason for this follows from Mertzman's opinion that the dead woman had borne a child before. In the family crisis of 1892, Lizzie and her mother were at loggerheads. Elizabeth was obviously upset by Lizzie's affair which had led to the firing. However, since Lizzie had been pregnant before, and never married, this opens up a whole new scenario that is universal in nature, a tragedy that has recurred for countless young women throughout human history. She had gotten pregnant out of wedlock, and we know she bore the child—we have Mertzman's authority on that. That means she most likely gave the child up for adoption, which is biologically and psychologically very traumatic for an already shaken young woman. The hormonal changes in the young mother's body are all-pervasive, and continue past delivery in the form of lactation and other changes. When the child is then abruptly torn from her, in the midst of a vast societal wave of disapproval, the young woman is traumatized. There is no mention of a father in the Wyllie household, which suggests the possibility of previous troubles (either Mr. Wyllie left his family, or perhaps he died, but there is no way this could not also have been traumatic). When Lizzie apparently again stumbled into the same error, we can understand how distraught Mrs. Wyllie would have been—enough to cause Lizzie to flee into exile with her aunt. It is undoubtedly this rift that John Longfield's letter refers to when he claims Lizzie is in Toronto and wants nothing more to do with her family. That is in a letter he sent from Cleveland to his wife. This indirectly and purposefully telegraphed a message to Mrs. Wyllie. This weird and unbelievable message also reached a Yellow Press eager for scandal.

The San Francisco Chronicle reports:[73] "Driven almost to distraction by worry and shame, Mrs. Elizabeth Wyllie of Detroit admitted this afternoon that it was her daughter Lizzie who was found dead..."

Mrs. Wyllie says her daughter eloped a month earlier with [John G. Longfield] of Detroit. Neither Lizzie nor Longfield had any money. She pins the date of Lizzie's disappearance at "five weeks ago last Monday [on or about Monday, Oct. 24] she went...downtown on an errand. She never returned." She had apparently said she was going to look for work, which one would expect on a Monday, and did not go alone. We need not take the hiatus as exactly thirty days, because it changes with plasticity from a month to five weeks, and might be a little longer. In Mrs. Wyllie's distraught frame of mind, exactitude would not be likely.

The article reports a somewhat disjointed story that on the Saturday before Lizzie's disappearance, a man called at the Wyllie house one afternoon to visit with Lizzie and her family, and to tell everyone goodbye. He said he was going south, likely to California, and he 'jocosely' told May Wyllie "I will be picking roses in California while your feet are freezing in Detroit." That man cannot have been Longfield, because he would have been thrown on his ear by May and Mrs. Wyllie. Much of Detroit probably knew the story of the three being fired from the bookbindery, except maybe Longfield's patient and gullible wife. More likely, the visitor was just an acquaintance of May Wyllie, and the reference to California was merely coincidence. However, the tone of the paper makes it sound as if there is more to the story (the man "also disappeared")[74] so there is a remote possibility it might have been the other man in the story—a lover or accomplice of Kate's who also appeared at the bank in Hamburg to help set up the $25 credit.

Mrs. Wyllie is described as 'prepossessing' and Lizzie was 'an attractive girl.' Kate Morgan's unappealing photograph suggested to contemporaries that she was not the same person, as we'll see.

Apparently the name L. Anderson Bernard reminded Mrs. Wyllie of her lost daughter. The initial L would stand for Lizzie, while Anderson is the name of her married sister in Grand Rapids. Just as the invented name must have sent signals to Spreckels, so it sent signals to Mrs. Wyllie in her mother's instinct that the worst had come to pass.

Regarding her receipt of the telegram describing the dead woman in Coronado, the article reads: "Mrs. Wyllie read the telegram as far as the mention of the two moles and then the paper dropped from her hands. 'My Lizzie; it's my Lizzie,' she sobbed repeatedly. 'What will become of me?' Not a word of reproach came from her lips upon the name of the dead girl." We of today must give enormous credence to this woman's belief that the dead person was her daughter.

We can construct a loose timeline for events from the clues here. Lizzie was in Los Angeles in October and November, and finally in San Diego during late November. Nobody noticed or mentioned she was pregnant, so she was probably not past the middle of her term. That means she was less than four or five months pregnant (at most). In turn, that suggests she became pregnant in either July or August. She would have noticed a missed period in, let's say, September, and at some point maybe some morning sickness. Having had a child before, the symptoms would be quite unmistakable to her. She would have noticed a second missed period in October. That was approximately the time when she, May, and Longfield were all fired from their jobs. It is possible that Lizzie (just before being fired) both logically argued with Longfield from the desperate situation in which she found herself, and emotionally harangued him because of strong hormonal surges. One can imagine the scandal and titillation that disrupted the strict Victorian work ethic, perhaps with all three persons storming back and forth with accusations, denials, demands, and angry refusals, and in the end they were all sacked.

So again…if Lizzie had been pregnant out of wedlock before, by her own irresponsibility, and had to give the child up for adoption, this would have been traumatic for her, as well as for her mother and sister. Mrs. Wyllie could not have failed to notice the signs that Lizzie was pregnant again. Lizzie took off for at least a week or two to stay with her Aunt Louisa on the other side of the Michigan peninsula. Mrs. Wyllie was no doubt on her war horse, and Longfield was setting up his own alibi in Cleveland or elsewhere, looking for work out of town and out of his wife's reach. Lizzie had a cooling off period, during which she probably cried a great deal, and Aunt Louisa gave her a stack of hankies to dry her tears.

This is how Lizzie ended up with two sets of hankies—some embroidered Lizzie Anderson, others Louisa Anderson. Deputy Coroner Stetson found the Lizzie hankies in Room 302 at the Del after her death, while Los Angeles Police found the Louisa hankies in the trunk from the L.A. Grants' house where Katie Logan had worked.

Day 12—Monday, Dec. 5, 1892

As the body lay in state in San Diego, the bank president in Hamburg, Iowa telegraphed to say he thought Mrs. Bernard's husband was named John. He had personally never met this John. Can this be a reference to John Longfield? Did Longfield or someone interacting with him make a slip of the tongue and give his real name, much as Lizzie blurted out hers in Los Angeles? It seems that the only really talented liar among the conspirators was Kate Morgan.

Day 13—Tuesday, Dec. 6, 1892

The San Diego Union claims[75] that it is now for certain that the dead girl is 'pretty Lizzie Wyllie' of Detroit.

Speculation has it that "Longfield was at Hamburg under an assumed name, and sent Lizzie the $25. As I have assumed here, the press back in 1892 already fastened on the theory that John Longfield was still in the picture. It seems fairly clear that he really wanted to get back to his wife and children, or he would not have continued the charade of searching for work in Cleveland. It almost has to be that Kate Morgan was stringing him along, in order to dangle him as a carrot before Lizzie. Kate had to get Lizzie to stay with the program, both at the L. A. Grants' and in Coronado. We know that Lizzie was under considerable duress (e.g., she was anxious to get papers signed in Los Angeles; she was unhappy about her husband, a gambler whose whereabouts she didn't know; and in Coronado she kept asking about her 'brother,' who could be none other than John Longfield, upon whom her life and her future hung, not to mention the fate of her unborn child).[76] To keep the attention of a sporting fellow like Longfield, who had been reckless enough to gamble his family and his job, which he lost, amid a reputation for unsavory activities, Kate Morgan had only two weapons (or carrots) in her arsenal. The first was the promise of great wealth to flow from her scheme against John Spreckels. The second was her undoubtedly equine sexual appetite, which obviously captivated John Longfield. I think Longfield went back East at least twice—the first time, to retrieve Lizzie's trunks and to plant the $25 credit in Hamburg; later, to pick up his job hunting charade, placate his wife from afar, and plant the disinformation his manipulative lover Kate Morgan wanted to target at Elizabeth Wyllie (that she would never see her daughter again, not because she lay dead in San Diego, but because somehow her pregnancy, insolvency, and lack of work skills or references had been solved, and she was living a life of bliss in Toronto—utterly absurd). When Lizzie met John on the train from Denver, he was no doubt returning from the East, with her trunks on board. He had no intention of seeing Lizzie, and was surprised when she boarded the train. Longfield's goal was to rejoin Kate Morgan and receive his rewards. In the heat of his disavowal of Lizzie, he stormed off the train and forgot to give her the three baggage claim checks.

⇛⇝

The San Francisco Chronicle reports[77] that staff at the Hotel del Coronado were impressed with the charm, education, and class of the woman who died at the hotel. They feel her knowledge of the fine hotels of San Francisco and Los Angeles could not be forthcoming from a factory girl only recently run away from Detroit.

In a separate article, the same paper reports that Mrs. Longfield sent her husband a letter in Cleveland on Saturday [Dec. 3]. As noted in the previous passages, John Longfield at this point was enamored of Kate Morgan, and would do anything for her; hence, the absurd letter saying Lizzie was alive and well in Toronto (across Lake Ontario from Detroit) and never wanted to see or contact her loving mother and sister again. This spurious letter alone puts a huge and irreparable crack into the entire mythos of the Kate Morgan saga as it has been commonly received.

Day 14—Wednesday, Dec. 7, 1892

The San Diego Union reports[78] that the undertaker has sent a photograph of the dead woman's face to Mrs. Wyllie in Detroit.

The mortuary noted the discrepancy that Lizzie had pierced ears, whereas the corpse did not.

The handkerchiefs did not read 'Lottie Anderson,' as previously reported, but 'Louisa Anderson'—the exact name of Lizzie's aunt in Grand Rapids, Michigan. This is no coincidence.

The article mentions that a telegram had come from [sender not named] the previous day, Dec. 6, swinging the weight back into the Bernard camp. Allegedly, a professional gambler named L. A. Bernard had recently come through Hamburg. It is remarkable that this man, who was for a time thought to be the deceased's husband, shared the same initials with his wife. Could they both be L. A. Bernard? The papers become entangled in the contradictions of this L.A. Bernard/G.L. Allen story, but the simple answer would be that an unknown outsider [Longfield?] posing as L. A. Bernard came to town, spoke with the bank manager (while accidentally blurting out his name was John), and set up the $25 credit with help from G. L. Allen (who may have been a real resident of the area). The bottom line to it is that the Hamburg bank reference would have lent credibility to Lottie A. Bernard's machinations in Coronado, had she not been dead by the time the money arrived. It seems quite possible that the Spreckels Machine were spreading rumors via the Yellow Press to set up the discredited Morgans as villains, just in case the true story of the blackmail were to leak out. Spreckels' agents clearly built a powerful defensive position, now that their nemesis was dead; its effectiveness is evident from history, and the fact that even in the twenty-first century, the smokescreen ghost story survives stronger than ever (a good marketing play for the local tourist trade). Spreckels owned the major newspapers in San Diego, *The San Diego Union* and *The Herald-Tribune*, which had the lead for most of the time in how this story was fed to national news media. These two papers had boots on the ground, and reporting resources in place, to do legwork no other paper could do, even assuming *The Los Angeles Times*, let's say, had sent a reporter down the coast for a few days.

∾❤∾

The San Francisco Chronicle opines that Miss Lizzie Wyllie of Detroit and Mrs. L. Anderson Bernard "were not the same person. The Wyllie girl is alive and well in Toronto and Mrs. Bernard is supposed to have been the wife of a Hamburg, Iowa gambler..." and "...As he promised in his dispatch of yesterday, Longfield, whose name has been associated with Miss Wyllie's disappearance, enclosed to his wife a letter from Miss Wyllie, dated Toronto, in which she says that she is not coming home... and indicates that Lizzie left home on account of trouble with her family."[79] So there we have it, again—a transparent ruse, but *cui bono*?

Is it Kate Morgan, working through John Longfield, to deflect attention from herself and onto the unidentified dead woman (Lizzie)? Or is it the Spreckels Machine, continuing to deflect attention away from the discarded Lizzie identification, to further bolster the Kate Morgan schema? The County Coroner's finding is that the dead woman is 'Lottie Anderson Bernard, a.k.a. Kate Morgan' once the 'lost' official transcript has been 'recovered' by clerk W. W. Whitson. [Again, if the county's intention had been to wait for release until the dead woman's identity was certain, they would not have 'lost' or 'misplaced' the document for that purpose, as has been suggested. They would have stated: "We are withholding release of the official transcript, pending final certainty about the dead woman's identity."]

If Kate Morgan were behind the letter, one benefit to her would be if she were to actually assume the dead girl's identity. This seems like a stretch, until we consider that aliases were Kate Morgan's stock in trade. In any case, it would benefit her if the dead woman were confirmed to be Kate Morgan, since her name had been dragged through the mud nationally and would be of no further use to her. Kate Morgan, as such, was ruined. She would have to assume an entirely new identity—but that was one of her major talents.

Day 15—Thursday, Dec. 8, 1892

The San Diego Union reports[80] that, based on the issue of the pierced ears, the dead woman was not Lizzie Wyllie. Lizzie had pierced ears and wore silver earrings, while the dead woman's ears were not pierced. As I have elaborated in the discussion of the pierced earlobes versus twin moles on the left cheek (see Nov. 29 in *Part IV: Solved!*), the twin moles must win out over the pierced earlobes. She was Lizzie, not Kate.

The only halfway viable story at this point is that told by G. L. Allen of Hamburg, Iowa. Allen says he was a schoolmate of a gambler named L. A. Bernard, whose wife lay ill in California. At her request [Gomer's] he wired $25 credit, without ever having met her. The San Diego papers, however, tend to be suspicious of Allen and not believe his story because of details that in themselves are convoluted and dubious. Odd, too, is the fact that then both husband and wife would have the same initials—LAB. Sounds like two imaginary rabbits pulled from the same cocked hat.

A Mrs. Florence S. Howard, of Orange, California, writes that the dead woman is one Josie Brown, 24, of Detroit—another of Kate Morgan's many aliases.

•••

A new theory now raises its head, that the dead woman was the missing Katie Logan of Los Angeles. *The Los Angeles Times* reports[81] that "young woman's trunk and baggage are...at Mrs. [L.A.] Grant's, No. 917 South Hill Street, where she was last seen. When she left, on the 23rd...she stated that she would be back in time for Thanksgiving dinner, but not a word has been heard from her since." The story relates that she arrived from Omaha about two months earlier [September or October]. She said her husband was a gambler, and she did not know what had become of him. She applied at several employment agencies. She first found work as a domestic at the R. M. Widneys', and then at the T. H. Hughes'. Lastly, she found employment at the L. A. Grants'.

The day before she left Los Angeles, she was anxious to get some papers signed, and appeared to be very worried about something. Those papers most likely had something to do with her campaign to help John Longfield divorce his wife and marry Lizzie.

She wore the ring and the black underclothes described as being on the body found in Coronado. She had two moles on her left cheek.

"She told several persons that her name was Lizzie, but that she liked the name of Kittie better, and that was the reason she adopted it."

So, newspapers are now leaning toward the theory that Lottie A. Bernard was really a domestic named Katie Logan, who had disappeared from Los Angeles the day before Lottie A. Bernard appeared in Coronado. The descriptions of the two women ("attractive," etc.) match, and we note again that 'Katie Logan' blurted out that her real name was Lizzie. We know that Lizzie came from Detroit, but Katie Logan was "well posted" in San Francisco, and knew all about the public places and the hotels, which shows she must have lived there—in other words, Kate Morgan had grilled her well on the long train ride from Detroit to Los Angeles. Lizzie, who—unlike Kate Morgan—was attractive and a stylish dresser, would easily have passed for an urbane and sophisticated woman with a little prepping. Witnesses said Katie Logan was "fairly well educated" and had traveled much, since her husband was a gambler.

Day 16—Friday, Dec. 9, 1892

The San Diego Union reports[82] that the dead woman is still unidentified. The feeling now is that she was not Lizzie Wyllie, who is said to be living with her lover John G. Longfield in Ontario, Canada. She is now thought to be the wife of Iowa gambler L. A. Bernard.

Actually, at this moment in time, as the Lottie A. Bernard and Lizzie personas fade from popular attention, three new personas are in play—Katie Logan, Josie Brown, and Mrs. L. A. Bernard (wife of L.A. Bernard, somewhat absurdly). But the game of identities is moving to its final gambit: Kate Morgan.

Los Angeles police open Katie Logan's trunk and find a number of artifacts. The trunk contains objects and papers belonging primarily to Kate Morgan, but also the Louisa Anderson hankies that could only have come from Lizzie Wyllie's aunt in Grand Rapids.

May we suppose that Kate Morgan, in order to keep her muddled understudy straight on names, gave her her own name (Katie, as in Katie Logan, from Kate Morgan) in the hope she wouldn't blurt out that her name was Lizzie, but she preferred to go by Kitty...er, make that Katie?

The trunk also contained a tin box marked 'Louise' or 'Louisa.'[83] There again is Lizzie's Aunt Louisa.

There are a number of photos, locks of hair, etc. all probably from Kate Morgan's family. Oddly, on the backs of several photos, names had been "carefully erased."

A letter from W. J. [W.T.] Farmer, Hanford, recommended Mrs. Morgan as an honorable and trustworthy woman. I would suggest that Kate Morgan made a forgery of this letter, addressed to Katie Logan, and had Lizzie use that copy to gain her first temp job in Los Angeles. This was her training period for the caper in Coronado a month later.

The trunk contained the cards of several ladies and their addresses, where most likely Kate Morgan [Katie Logan] had worked: Mrs. J. H. McDonough of San Rafael; Mrs. M. R. Abbott of San Francisco; and Mrs. Ottinger of San Francisco. I would suggest that Kate Morgan spent some time working under who knows what fake name in San Francisco. There is no evidence she ever worked in the Spreckels household, but she would have heard stories from women who had, and quite possibly met a woman who had had an affair with Spreckels and had a packet of love letters—or the whole thing may have been at yet more of a remove—for example, a servant might have come across a packet of love letters while working at the Spreckels home, and stolen them for a lark—until Kate Morgan got her mitts on them and hatched a blackmail scheme.

The reporter questions whether the 'cabinet size photo' of a rather plain, even gross Mrs. Morgan could match the description of the 'Beautiful Stranger.' Whatever her sexual prowess that enslaved the already randy John Longfield, Kate Morgan and the dead woman were not the same person. Nevertheless, the identification now became the final one that appeared on the death certificate and would remain attached to the story until the 21st Century: Kate Morgan.

Day 17—Saturday, Dec. 10, 1892

The San Diego Union throws doubt on the Kate Morgan identification, affirming that the photograph of Mrs. Morgan in Los Angeles cannot fit the description of the Coronado suicide. The paper opines that the contents of the trunk—in which all names, addresses, and other personal information had been destroyed—proved that she wanted to conceal her identity.[84] How very much is the devious and scheming hand of Kate Morgan evident in all this!

Day 18—Sunday, Dec. 11, 1892

The San Diego Union reports[85] that a Mr. A. D. Swarts of Los Angeles
had contacted the coroner's office in San Diego to affirm the Kate Morgan
identification. Mr. Swarts may be on the level, or he may be a plant of the
Spreckels Machine, which has an interest in tarnishing the dead woman's
reputation to further defuse the threat to John Spreckels.

    The three trunks at the San Diego baggage depot (image: Grand Union
depot, demolished 1914, replaced by Santa Fe Depot) have been claimed
"by the owners" and this removes "any remaining doubt" that the dead
woman was Mrs. Kate Morgan. Indeed, John Spreckels probably did not
own the baggage depot outright, or Lizzie's three trunks would already
have disappeared. Most likely the Santa Fe Railroad owned the depot, and
was under injunction by local police to leave the trunks locked until there
could be a legal writ. For local authorities to open the trunks—and find a
trail of effects leading backward to Lizzie and Detroit—would have
opened the possibility of reviving elements of Kate Morgan's blackmail
scheme, thereby putting John Spreckels once again at risk. The three trunks
were a loose end. It's possible that Kate Morgan got the claim checks from
John, and paid a man with a donkey cart to pick them up so they could be
disposed of—burned, thrown into the ocean, buried in a distant canyon.
More likely, the Spreckels Machine created some fake checks and hauled
the trunks off, again for disposal. Likewise, the telegram or letter, or
however else Kate communicated the Lottie A. Bernard threat to John
Spreckels, ended up in oblivion. The end result is that history has been
handed an enigmatic and meaningless Swiss cheese of disjointed clues

pointing to a supposedly disreputable couple of petty criminals from Iowa, who cheated card players on trains...and a ghost story that lives on in opaque mystery at the Hotel del Coronado.

Day 19—Monday, Dec. 12, 1892

The San Diego Union reports[86] that Kate's grandfather, Joe Chandler, of Riverton, Iowa, sent a telegram to the undertaker, Johnson & Company of San Diego. "Your telegram received regarding Kate Morgan, nee Farmer. Bury her and send me statement.—J. W. Chandler." It is clear Mr. Chandler was at the end of his rope with his niece, and with good reason. Nobody would be in a better position than Chandler to know what a dark spirit she really was. Although Kate's relatives and acquaintances concurred that she was definitely not the type to commit suicide, the world now accepts the story that the dead woman was Kate Morgan. Nobody even raises the issue that the owner of the Hotel del Coronado was John Spreckels, and that there actually might be a reasonable explanation, however far-fetched.

Day 20—Tuesday, Dec. 13, 1892

No news.

Day 21—Wednesday, Dec. 14, 1892 (Funeral and Burial)

After the funeral, police finally hear from Kate's uncle in Hanford, W. T. Farmer, who says Kate had no cause for suicide. Farmer implies that, if the body was indeed hers (so there is still doubt), something else caused her death. He wrote that her husband, Thomas E. Morgan (Tom Morgan) was traveling on business for a manufacturing company, and his home was in Hamburg, Iowa. Farmer knew them for many years, and protested he did not believe Kate Morgan would have committed suicide—so there must be a mistake about the identity pinned on the corpse. The reporter (employed by *The San Diego Union*, one of John Spreckels' newspapers) presses his conviction that it was Kate Morgan, and that she did commit suicide. The reporter does (conveniently) allow that a number of mysteries about the case may never be answered.

Part V. Lottiepedia

(Concordance A-Z)

Guide to the Concordance:

This alphabetic concordance is an encyclopedic reference for some of the salient people, places, and topics in my book. My principal source is the Hotel del Coronado's official and well-researched Heritage Department book (Beautiful Stranger: The Ghost of Kate Morgan and the Hotel del Coronado, ISBN 091625173X and ISBN 9780916251737, edition of 2002, available in bookstores and online). Usually, I reference at least the first page ('[page number]') on which a word occurs, but some words occur several times in the book. To really understand my conjecture in full, please read both my book and the Hotel Del's official book, and see the multitude of clues buried in plain sight in the latter. The hotel's book, however, does not offer a sufficient contextual framework of events beyond the Lottie A. Bernard story, showing the connections with Spreckels and the Hawai'ian monarchy, among the many contemporaneous factors so important to the story. I frequently use the acronym LAB (Lottie Anderson Bernard) in reference to the woman who died. Page numbers for Beautiful Stranger (HD for Heritage Department or Hotel Del) may be accompanied by closer reference for either Upper Left, Middle Left, Lower Left, Upper Right, Middle Right, or Lower Right—e.g., [HD63UL] would mean 'Heritage Dept. page 63 upper left;' similarly: [HD5ML] [HD9LL] [HD13MR] [HD22UR] [HD79LR]. References within this book (Dead Move: Kate Morgan and the Haunting Mystery of Coronado, Fourth Edition) are noted [DM], followed by a page number if practicable.

Anderson:

Lizzie's aunt in Grand Rapids was Louisa Anderson. The name Lottie Anderson Bernard gave as her alleged brother's was Dr. Anderson, 'a practicing physician in Indianapolis' [HD31UL]. LAB may have told Gomer her 'brother's' name was Dr. M. C. Anderson [HD29UL]. Hankies with the name (Louise or) Louisa Anderson [HD70LL] were found in Kate Morgan's trunk at the L.A. Grants' home in Los Angeles, where Katie

Logan (another fake name) worked briefly as a temporary housemaid. The contents of this trunk tie the two women (Lizzie Wyllie and Kate Morgan) together, along with 'Katie Logan' blurting out that her real name was Lizzie.

Bernard:

Fake name given by the Beautiful Stranger while staying at the Hotel del Coronado [HD1UL]. Full name: Lottie Anderson Bernard. Anderson was the name of Lizzie's aunt in Grand Rapids [HD].

NOTE: (6/25/2012) Increasingly, I have to wonder if the choice of names (Lottie or Charlotte Bernard) was random, or if it actually was the name of a woman Spreckels would recognize as a potential blackmail candidate. The Anderson middle name most likely relates to Lizzie's Aunt Louisa Anderson in Grand Rapids, Michigan. Like Katie Logan, it sounds like a name Kate Morgan made up to comfort and reassure poor Lizzie. Will future research determine that there was a domestic or other woman in the orbit of John D. Spreckels (or his brother Adolph?) in San Francisco, who could be a potential source of embarrassment and, in Kate Morgan's hopes, lead to a payoff to avoid scandal?

brother:

Neither Kate Morgan nor Lizzie Wyllie had a brother in real life. Kate had no siblings, and Lizzie had one sister named May who lived with Lizzie and her mother (Elizabeth) in Detroit, possibly at an address given in the 1890 census (237 Fifth Street, Detroit [DM]). Kate Morgan, while pulling her scams, always claimed to have a brother who was a doctor, hovering somewhere nearby. I believe she taught Lizzie how to be an impersonator, and the fake 'Dr. Anderson' (Lottie A. Bernard's alleged brother) fit the bill. LAB was clearly obsessed with his contacting her, which he never did. He was probably either her lover (John Longfield, who had split angrily from her in the train incident at Orange) or possibly even a local abortion specialist being secretly retained to help her if anything went wrong, per Stetson's quote [HD35LL] "...send for the doctor..." (my italics). Could this even have been the house physician [HD29LL,UR], who had gone hunting early that day [HD31UL], presumably on North Island, despite the previous night's storm? She does make reference to the man on the train as her 'brother' [HD2LL], so most likely it was John Longfield—the man who had 'ruined' her, and who she desperately hoped would leave his wife and children to marry her—which shows again how air-headed poor Lizzie really was, and how Kate Morgan probably had strung her along with such fantasies.

Brown, Josie:

One of Kate Morgan's aliases. Reported by a lady in Anaheim.

doctor:

Kate Morgan had a history of using aliases in various cities, and stating that she had a brother who was a doctor, practicing in various other cities, who was however hovering somewhere nearby, apparently ready to come to her rescue if needed. This appears to have been partly a claim to some respectability (being of a family that produced a respected physician) and a veiled threat (that she had a concerned and capable man ready to come to her aid if needed).

embalming:

It can be inferred that the body was embalmed,[87] for she lay in state in a public room at Johnson & Company for about two weeks, during which she became a national *cause célèbre* of the Yellow Press, with breathless daily or even hourly telegraph reports emanating from San Diego.

The body's hair was cropped, and a police sketch was sent abroad in an effort to get someone to identify her.

Detroit:

Lizzie's home city [HD1]. Given by Lottie A. Bernard as her home city signing in to the hotel register [HD54]. Home of John Longfield, and the Wyllie family (Lizzie's mother Elizabeth and sister May).

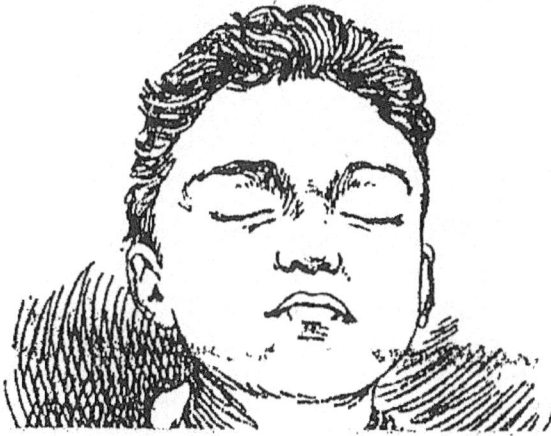

Since it was at first assumed she was Mrs. Lottie Bernard, and there was only a matter of locating Mr. Bernard (who did not exist, because the name was a false alias), the sketch probably was not made until several days after her death. After lying on the frigid steps for hours, then being carried across to the city (was she packed in ice? Nobody today knows for sure how the body was handled), the cadaver was treated at Johnson & Company. The embalming process is performed in various ways, but generally serves to preserve the body in as lifelike a condition as possible. Some of the body's processes disappear with death and the removal of inner organs. Other processes, pertaining to the skin, like hair growth and nail growth, may continue for a time. Common chemicals used by morticians in Lottie Bernard's time included arsenic and formaldehyde.[88] While these chemicals have slightly different effects, in common they cause the death of bacteria that cause flesh to break down. Among the most noticeable changes in the body after death is rigor mortis, the stiffening of the muscles that may cause contortions, accompanied by a loss of water that causes the body to shrink. Decomposition and putrefaction cause the breakdown of proteins through hydrolysis and anaerobic bacterial processes, resulting in foul-smelling liquids called cadaverine and putrescine. Within two to four weeks, the individual's face becomes unrecognizable. There are no known photographs of the dead woman. There is just the police sketch, which must have been done when a search failed to turn up Mr. Bernard or any other relatives or friends of the deceased. The sketch was done at some point between November 30 (day of the coroner's inquest) and December 14 (probable day of her funeral and burial).

gun:

According to a firearms expert I consulted, and my own Web browsing, the American Bulldog revolver of the 1890s was not so much a brand as a generic type of handgun. The standard British Army revolver of the 1870s was the .45 Webley. A civilian knockoff called the British Bulldog was popular. Foreign copies included the Belgian Bulldog and the American Bulldog. The American Bulldog type consisted of a variety of calibers and models, which today would be classified as a 'suicide special' or a 'Saturday night special' or even a 'throwaway' on the low end. No wonder that testimony indicates it had rust on it. Its basic model was a .32 caliber six shot revolver, which was actually a smaller handgun for the times. It had a standard grip, and a short barrel. The range of calibers and dimensions varied all the way up to the .44 that LAB used to shoot herself. Gun dealer Chick says [HD32UL] he sold LAB a .44 American Bulldog. Physician/surgeon B.F. Mertzman says [HD23LL] he estimates the round to have been in the range of .38 to .40. This putative discrepancy was later (1980s) cited as possible grounds for a framed murder, in that the bullet allegedly did not match the gun. But the round taken from her skull had been damaged during the shooting, obviously, and a 1980s review of the case did not find sufficient grounds to review or overturn the 1892 jury finding of suicide. While one can't 100% rule out the possibility of murder, the fact that she went into town to purchase a gun that most likely killed her considerably weakens any supposition of murder. That's because she herself introduced a gun into the equation, and suicide is the simplest way to explain the causative arc from that purchase, across her obvious debility and depression, to her ultimate demise. The electrician Cone [HD18UR] who first found the body describes the gun as 'large.' A point of detail is in order here. The gun itself would have been considered relatively light for the time period. However, the .44 caliber introduces a new variable. Because of the size of the round, the highly unusual cylinder was able to contain only five shots. The cylinder still looked enlarged compared to the .32 for which the generic gun was designed. So most likely what Cone saw was not a really 'large' handgun, but a somewhat grotesque .44 handgun whose swollen-looking cylinder midsection looked out of place between the standard grip and short barrel designed for the .32 models.

husband:

LAB signs in at the Hotel del Coronado as Mrs. Lottie Anderson Bernard, yet she seems to devote her anxieties to waiting for her alleged brother ('Dr. Anderson'), not her alleged husband ('Mr. Bernard')—e.g.

when chief hotel clerk Gomer questions her [HD29LR] about her finances and resources. It is interesting that this probably makes LAB's alleged maiden name Anderson, the name of Lizzie's aunt in Grand Rapids. More interesting is the fact that she does not seem concerned about her husband—though the man who angrily left her on the train at Orange was most likely in fact not a 'husband,' but Lizzie's lover John Longfield. It was most likely Longfield that she kept hoping to hear from, and his failure to contact her seems a plausible motive for suicide [DM179], in the further context of her self-medication, guilt about harming her fetus, and guilt about disappointing her mother and sister.

Fibs:

Lizzie (Mrs. Katie Logan, Mrs. Lottie Bernard) lets slip a series of moments in which we glimpse her airheaded struggle with a situation that was clearly over her head. The first and most glaring is when she tells a fellow housekeeper in Los Angeles that her name is really Lizzie, then quickly corrects herself and gets even her fake name wrong (Kittie, Katie). Another such moment is, as the clerk is signing her in, when she tells him she is Miss Lottie Bernard, and quickly corrects it to Mrs.—which is caught in the clerk's writing 'Mis' instead of 'Miss' or 'Mrs.' Another moment is when, on Monday November 28, Gomer comes to ask about her finances, and she abruptly changes her lie from 'neuralgia' to terminal stomach cancer. There is something child-like, blatant, almost comical, awkward, and transparent about all these fibs. Her capacity for self-delusion is evident from the invitation she sent herself from two prominent stage actresses of national fame.

Her instinct to fib is evident from the fact that she told Fosdick she was going into town to get her baggage, when in reality she was going to buy a gun; she didn't need to say anything; but he pressed her with good advice regarding the coming storm and her weak condition, and she had to make up something to show it was imperative that she make the trip.

Friends:

At the inquest, the Coroner asks his assistant, Stetson, if there was "No trace of her friends?" [HD35LR]. This may be an innocent phrasing, but it does raise the question—since she was alone the whole time, why this reference to 'friends'? Why not 'friend' instead of the plural? If one believes the entire inquest was rigged, a hasty affair serving the interests of Spreckels, and if the Coroner (who was absent on the morning the body was found, perhaps just as the house physician happened to be away

hunting [HD31UL]) knew more than he was saying, it sounds like he may
have led the witness. It is an odd question that seems to open the door to
the possibility that, as my book suggests [DM], the Spreckels Machine
kept tabs on LAB and knew she had accomplices.

hankies:

Often, the little details loom surprisingly large in a situation like this.
There are several references to hankies in this story. At the Coroner's
Inquest, Coroner asks Stetson: "What is the name on the handkerchiefs?"[89]
(He means those found in the dead woman's room by Asst Coroner
Stetson.) Stetson says: "Little, I think it is, I cannot quite make it out, but
the last name is Anderson." Consider that nobody knew her name was not
Lottie A. Bernard at this point, and a nationwide search was on for both the
purported Dr. Anderson (brother), as well as the purported Mr. Bernard
(husband). We know that in a week or so, the corpse would be I.D.'d as
Lizzie Wyllie, and a few days later that choice would change to Kate
Morgan (on flimsy pretext). So we have Stetson innocently saying the
blurry first name on the faded hankie looks to him like *Little*, when in fact
that looks surprisingly like *Lizzie*. The opening capital *L* and small *i* are the
same, followed by a double consonant—a Victorian *zz* with a bar through
each *z* could easily look like a pair of *t*'s—followed by a small *l* or a small
t (again, the dot on the *i* could easily fade so the letter looks like an *l* with a
faint gap); and the final letters *e* are the same.

Stetson says with certainty that the last name is Anderson. Remember
that Lizzie's aunt in Grand Rapids is Louisa (or Louise, *q.v.*) Anderson,
which happens to be the name embroidered on the hankies found in Kate
Morgan's trunk at the L.A. Grants' home in Los Angeles (where I believe
Kate Morgan was training Lizzie to become a competent impostor, under
the name Katie Logan, preparing her for her coming role as LAB in
Coronado; despite the fact that she blurts out that her real name is Lizzie);
and the artifacts in the L.A. Grant trunk strongly help tie the two women
(Kate Morgan and Lizzie Wyllie) together.

There is a further tantalizing mystery about the hankies in her hotel
room. The simple case is that the blurred first name is Louisa (again,
similar to *Little*, but less so than *Lizzie*). In that case, Stetson is holding
simply a few more of the Louisa Anderson hankies Lizzie probably
borrowed during huge crying spells while staying with her aunt in Grand
Rapids. If in fact, however, the complete name really was *Lizzie Anderson*,
this raises an intriguing possibility. We know Lizzie as Lizzie Wyllie,
because that's how it was used in the popular press. Lizzie's aunt's
(Lizzie's mother Elizabeth's sister) in Grand Rapids is Louisa Anderson.

The fact that there were hankies embroidered both 'Lizzie Anderson' and 'Louisa Anderson' raises an interesting new dimension. Is it possible that Anderson was Louisa's maiden name? Can it be that Elizabeth Anderson married a man named Wyllie, who died sometime before 1892? And that her sister Louisa Anderson married a man whose name we do not know, but the names on the hankies were embroidered long before Elizabeth and Louisa grew to maturity and married? The long time span would account for the hankies both in the trunk in Los Angeles, and in the hotel room in Coronado, being almost unreadable. All we really need to know for our Coronado mystery is that Lizzie's hankies were found both in the trunk and in the hotel room, which makes her the dead woman in Coronado and ties her firmly in with Kate Morgan, so the two women were working together. Lizzie's outburst about her name suggests Katie Logan was Lizzie Wyllie, the gullible and pretty young runaway from Detroit in Kate Morgan's tutelage.

There is yet another hypothesis regarding the Lizzie Anderson hankies (if that's how the embroidery really read). Could it be that Lizzie's mother, Elizabeth Wyllie, had the maiden name of Elizabeth Anderson, went by Lizzie also in her youth, and simply gave some hankies embroidered with that name to her daughter? That would account for the age and fading of the hankies found in Room 302 at the Hotel Del in 1892. Again, there is nothing pointing to Kate Morgan in any of this, but each Anderson hypothesis points to Lizzie as having been the woman who died at the Hotel Del.

Jones, Joseph:

Joseph A. Jones[90] of Boston or Joseph E. Jones[91] of Boston was not called to testify at the inquest, but he mentioned[92] to a bellman at the Hotel Del that he recognized the woman who signed in before him, LAB, as having been on a train with him.

Despite the remarkable coincidence this invokes, I tend to take Jones at face value. Here is a man, Bostonian in origin, who happens to be (we assume) on a business trip. He is on a train from Denver, Colorado, to Orange, California, and late in that trip he notices a woman arguing with a man on the train.[93] Jones is sitting in the same railcar when this occurs. It is most important to note in his statement that he did not notice them until the train got near the Pacific coast[94], because this tends to corroborate my theory that Lizzie ('Katie Logan') during the 'Missing Day' made this significant detour that led somehow to the loss of her baggage claim tickets. Whether it was Kate Morgan, or Lizzie Wyllie was 'Katie Logan' in Los Angeles, is immaterial—either way, she mysteriously appeared on a westbound train from Denver to Orange, when she should have been on a southbound train from Los Angeles to San Diego.

If we take Jones at face value (despite the coincidence that he was in a rail car with 'Lottie A. Bernard' on the way from Denver to Orange, and later signed in after she did at the Hotel del Coronado) then the woman on the train from Denver to Orange and the woman who signed in at the Hotel Del were the same person. I cannot, at this writing, imagine Jones to be either another concoction of Kate Morgan, or a plant of the Spreckels Machine to sow disrepute upon the conspirators.

Jones is an ephemeral character in this story. It's not known to which bellman he told his tale. He was not summoned to testify at the coroner's inquest—because, according to the bellman, he was averse to testifying, and thus did not reveal his information until after the inquest. Was he a man with secrets he was afraid would become known, or was he just too busy to get involved? Did those secrets have anything to do with the Beautiful Stranger, or was he merely a man in a hurry, who did not want to get bogged down in a criminal case that had no bearing on his business interests? Jones vanishes into history as ephemerally as he briefly appears, second-hand. He says the man with whom Lottie Bernard argued on the train was 'well-dressed,' which does support the notion he was John Longfield, who was known as a ladies' man in Detroit.

I believe Lottie Bernard was on her way from the L.A. Grants' house in Los Angeles to meet her fate in the San Diego area, but knew John Longfield would be on the train from Denver, so she boarded somewhere east of Orange. That could have been anywhere east of Anaheim. She pleaded with him until he stormed off the train at Orange (presumably to link up with Kate Morgan, with whom I believe he was by then sexually intimate) while LAB rode westward to Anaheim, and then changed trains to ride south to San Diego. Somehow, in that process, Longfield must have pocketed the checks (receipts) for her three trunks, which wound up in San Diego, and which she could not retrieve without the tickets. Perhaps, for some reason, he was bringing her trunks to her on the train by a huge detour, since the trunk at the L.A. Grant house (where LAB had worked and lived in as Katie Logan) belonged to Kate Morgan.

Kate Morgan:

A grifter from Iowa, often mistakenly thought of as the Beautiful Stranger who lay dead at the Hotel del Coronado 28-29 November 1892. My analysis clearly shows that she was instead the organizer of the blackmail plot, in whose failure Lizzie Wyllie died of a self-inflicted gunshot to the head.

A photograph (shown), allegedly of Kate Morgan, has circulated on the Internet. If this is Kate Morgan, she does not resemble the victim in the police sketch (see Embalming), who was Lizzie Wyllie. Lizzie's mother agreed that the dead girl's sketch represented her missing daughter. Hotel guests and employees stated that a photo they were shown of Kate Morgan (unavailable; presumably similar to the photo at right), did not resemble the Beautiful Stranger they had admired in life.

Katie Logan:

An alias that we probably all agree was invented by Kate Morgan. The traditional view is that Kate Morgan used the name Katie Logan while posing as a temporary domestic worker at contractor L. A. Grant's house in Los Angeles. My view is that Kate Morgan was training Lizzie Wyllie for the big impersonation (Lottie A. Bernard) at the Hotel Del, and Lizzie was the woman posing as Katie Logan at the L. A. Grants'. At one point, Katie Logan tells a co-worker that her real name is Lizzie.[95] It appears she blurted this out and quickly corrected herself, saying she preferred Kittie, then amended that to Katie. Presumably, the other woman, who reported this to police later, would have no reason to mistake the woman she knew as Katie for someone named Kittie, so most likely 'Kittie' is another of Lizzie's muddle-headed fumbles and clumsy fibs.

Another huge clue is the fact that, in Kate Morgan's trunk at the L.A. Grant house, was found a box labeled Louisa Anderson. That is the name of Lizzie's aunt in Grand Rapids, Michigan. Also found in the trunk were hankies with the name Louisa Anderson embroidered. But there was a photo of Kate Morgan as well, all of which proves beyond a reasonable doubt that Kate Morgan and Lizzie Wyllie were together in the plot—first, impersonating the fictitious Katie Logan in Los Angeles, and secondly impersonating Lottie A. Bernard in Coronado.

Missing Day:

Commentators have cited a 'missing 24 hours' between November 23 and 24, which is far longer than the short train ride it should have taken Lottie A. Bernard to arrive in San Diego from Los Angeles.

The resolution of the Lottie A. Bernard mystery does, for several reasons, suggest she took a time-consuming side trip, by rail, from Los Angeles to Orange, and from Orange to Anaheim, and thence to San Diego. The side trip did not require exactly 24 hours, but would have exhausted the better part of a day.

A passenger from Boston, Joseph E. Jones, was on the train that brought John back West from Iowa. In Iowa, Longfield had left a smallish sum ($25) with a bank manager, along with a tall tale that it was in case the money were needed by his school chum's ailing wife in Coronado. Lizzie had just left the L. A. Grant household on her way to San Diego. By now, she had a serious inkling that things were not all as Kate described them about John, but she did not yet blame Kate for being a liar and manipulator. Knowing that the train was to arrive in Anaheim, Lizzie traveled several hours east and met the train in Orange. From Orange to Anaheim, she pleaded and argued with a reticent John Longfield to marry her in Coronado. She was getting cold feet about Kate's plot, and thought it would be so much simpler if John were to rescue her and marry her. But John was following Kate's orders and demurred. The result was a rising argument that ended with John storming from the train in Anaheim. It was the last time he and Lizzie would ever see each other, and the mysterious passenger Jones would describe it to bellmen at the hotel a few days later—though he avoided attending the Coroner's inquest for some reason—perhaps connected with a cover-up by the Spreckels Machine.

Why did it take the woman more than a day to make the two-hour train trip from Los Angeles to San Diego? She left her employer, L.A. Grant, in Los Angeles on November 23rd, and arrives in Coronado on the afternoon of the next day. For all we know, she may have gone shopping—except that a witness, Joseph E. Jones of Boston, told a bellman at the Hotel Del that he recognized the mystery woman at the hotel as being the same woman he had seen on the train from Denver the day before, having a loud argument with a man who stormed off the train at Orange. What was Lottie A. Bernard doing on a train from east to west at a time when she logically would have been on a different train going from north to south? I have pieced together a plausible explanation—she was making a desperate bid to regain the affections of the man she loved, who was in the process of dumping her and betraying her in Kate Morgan's plot to blackmail John Spreckels. She traveled south from Los Angeles, then traveled a brief distance east to intercept John Longfield. She pleaded with him on the brief trip west to Orange, but his rejection of her sounded like a quarrel to the witness, Jones. Longfield jumped off the train at Orange and strode off into history, never to see her again. She continued her fateful journey south to San Diego and to her doom.

Pregnancy

The leading medical authority in San Diego, Dr. B. F. Mertzman, was not allowed to autopsy the dead woman, but he examined the body for about a half hour on the morning after she died, in other words about 24 hours after her body was found, and he stated with certainty,[96-97] from his experience as a physician and surgeon, that (a) she was pregnant (which puts her anywhere from about the first or second month, when vaginal changes would start becoming apparent, to around the fifth month (*q.v.*) when her pregnancy would have been obvious to observers, and nobody who met her indicated any inkling that she might be gravid); (b) she was taking what Mertzman called "terrible medicines" to induce a miscarriage; and (c) she had borne at least one child in the past.

On Saturday, Nov. 26, Lottie (Lizzie) sent bellman Harry West on an enigmatic quest for an empty pint bottle and a sponge from the hotel drugstore.[98] It has been common practice since ancient Egyptian times for women to use a pessary, or sponge filled with poisons, to induce a miscarriage. The empty pint bottle (and this is all speculation, but quite provocative) could have been used to mix medicines. Some of the abortifacients used in ancient times in pessaries (vaginal suppositories, still used today but with modern medicines) included the herb pennyroyal, which functions as a natural contraceptive.

Sponge

See Pregnancy.

Stingaree

One of the most notorious red light districts on the West Coast, located approximately between today's Market (then H) Street and K Street (near the downtown baseball field today) and between Fifth Street (today's Fifth Avenue) and Second Street (today's Second Avenue). The Stingaree got its name from the stingray, a flat fish with a razor-sharp, poisonous quill for a tail. It likes to sleep in the warm, shallow waters after flapping to cover itself with sand. Lifeguards warn persons wading near shore make noise and splash water to wake the sleeping rays, which then scamper off. Many a wader has gotten an excruciatingly pierced foot requiring weeks of healing. Fatalities (like Steve Irwin, killed by the much larger Australian stingray than the pelagic stingray of San Diego) are rare, but they do occur.[99] The Stingaree was rife with prostitution, gambling, and drug abuse including heroin and opium. Shootings and stabbings were frequent. The saying was that "you could get stung as badly in the Stingaree as in the Bay." Ironically, City Hall and the police headquarters were located at 5th and G Streets near the heart of the district. Wyatt Earp ran four gambling establishments here when our Beautiful Stranger appeared on the scene.

Trunks:

Two sets of luggage are in play. One is a trunk (belonging to Kate Morgan) at the L.A. Grants' house in Los Angeles, and containing artifacts of both Lizzie Wyllie and Kate Morgan [HD70]. The other is a set of three trunks belonging to LAB, kept at the baggage terminal near the railroad station at the foot of D Street (today's West Broadway, and the current Santa Fe Depot occupies almost exactly the same spot as the old station). LAB arrived in San Diego probably late morning to noon on Thanksgiving Day, Thursday, November 24, 1892. Thanksgiving was not the huge holiday it is today, and businesses were open. LAB tried to collect her trunks, but the baggage bureaucrats refused to turn them over because she did not have her tickets. She (Lizzie) says her 'brother'[100] had kept the 'checks' when they separated at Orange.

This cleanly links to the observation by Joseph Jones of Boston that he witnessed an argument between the woman who checked into the Hotel Del just before him as 'Lottie A. Bernard' and an unknown man on the Denver to Orange rail line, who Jones suspected was romantically involved with the woman. The baggage clerk refused to release the three trunks to her because she did not have the claim checks—and probably out of Victorian prejudice against an attractive young woman traveling alone. In any case, it appears that Lottie A. Bernard (who I believe was Lizzie Wyllie, not Kate Morgan) was traveling with three trunks.

Kate Morgan was traveling with one trunk, which ended up at the L.A. Grant house in Los Angeles. We have the testimony of Kate (nee Farmer) Morgan's uncle in the Hanford and Visalia areas near San Francisco (Farmer), who wrote to Los Angeles Police Chief Glass to protest any notion that his niece, Kate Morgan, was in a mindset to commit suicide.

Farmer says that she was in good spirits and (here's the kicker) "traveling with one flat-top trunk, two leather satchels, and a lady's gold watch."[101]

Meanwhile, the woman working for the L.A. Grants in Los Angeles, 'Katie Logan,' had a single trunk with her. This trunk stayed closed until well into December, when Los Angeles detectives finally opened it—and found a mix of possessions belonging to both Kate Morgan and Lizzie Wyllie. This is a new interpretation, because until now the contents of the trunk in Los Angeles were confusingly considered to lean toward an I.D. of 'Katie Logan' as Kate Morgan. My interpretation is that 'Katie Logan' was actually Lizzie Wyllie, whom Kate Morgan was giving a crash course in impersonations in preparation for her cameo role in the blackmail of John Spreckels, owner of the Hotel del Coronado—which would go horribly wrong.

So the matter of travel trunks boils down to this. Lizzie Wyllie had left Detroit, in the company of her lover John Longfield, with three trunks containing all her earthly possessions. Kate Morgan, meanwhile, was traveling with one trunk and most likely a lover —possibly her husband, Tom Morgan, but it is very likely she was getting romantically involved with Lizzie's paramour John Longfield—the latter, because he covers for her by sending a bogus account from Cleveland to his wife, saying 'Lizzie' was in Toronto.[102] I believe this story is false, and that, while Lizzie lay dead in San Diego, Kate Morgan was very much alive, assumed Lizzie's persona, and Kate may already have joined Longfield in Cleveland when he sent the letter to his gullible wife, to throw police and Lizzie's family off the trail. How long Kate and Longfield would have been together is anyone's guess, but I would surmise they tired of each other and he went back to his family in Detroit.

There is no way Kate Morgan's three Hanford pieces of luggage (a trunk and two leather satchels) can be twisted into being the three travel trunks stored at the baggage depot in San Diego. Therefore, we have compelling evidence that Kate Morgan was traveling with one trunk, which wound up at the L.A. Grant home in Los Angeles (with materials or props inside belonging to both Kate Morgan and Lizzie Wyllie), and that Lizzie Wyllie (who I surmise was both 'Katie Logan' and 'Lottie A. Bernard') arrived in San Diego with three trunks. By process of elimination, if Kate Morgan was traveling with one trunk, then the three trunks had to belong to the other woman in the case, Lizzie Wyllie.

Victorian culture:

She would have been just another nameless, faceless victim of random violence, had she not become an icon, a saint of Victorian melodrama and morbid sentiment (calling to mind the international hysteria over the life and passing of Little Nell, heroine of Charles Dickens' *The Little Curiosity Shop*, 1841, which was originally published in newspaper installments that were ferried across the Atlantic in mail ships, and which caused mobs on the Boston waterfront to riot as they cried "Is Little Nell dead? Is Little Nell dead?"[103] before the arriving ship could even dock with the latest episode on board).

The generic motif that so aroused the Victorian sentiment seems to center around an impeccably, heroically virtuous and angelically beautiful young female who is laid low by circumstance and the evil deeds of others, who violate her trust and sanctity, so that she finally dies in an orgiastic vision like that captured in the paintings of the Pre-Raphaelite[104] images like the famed Ophelia drowning (*Ophelia*[105] John Everett Millais, 1851-52, Tate Collection). The painting depicts a fully clothed beautiful young woman floating in water, with a dazed expression and half-closed eyes, while her pale hands are raised, palms up, in a gesture of limp and delicate surrender or supplication. Drawing upon the tragic character of Ophelia, Hamlet's love interest in the eponymous Shakespearean play, the painting has her mouthing vague snatches of happily remembered songs as her consciousness fades, and her clothing slowly fills with water and draws her under. We might consider this an absurd exaggeration of overblown sentiment, except that it is canonical as described in Act 4 Scene 7, Queen Gertrude's monologue[106] that begins "There is a willow grows aslant a brook..." Having been rejected in love by the angry and irrational Hamlet, and told to "get thee to a nunnery," the poor girl loses her mind, climbs into a tree—while crowned with an orchid garland—in a beautiful meadow (captured over five months' work by Millais, and as well remembered for its detail and beauty as the image of 19-year-old model Elizabeth Siddal), and accidentally falls to her death by drowning. To highlight the underlying realities of daily life that produced this phantasmagoria, the painter spent five months in a hut by a river, tormented by 'muscular' flies as he wryly called them; he was threatened by the local beadle with legal action for trespass; and, having painted the river scene, when he later inserted the scene of the drowning woman, he had his model posing in a warm bathtub at his apartment, but became so intent on his work that he let the candles go out under the tub, the water grew chill, and she caught a cold, for which Elizabeth Siddal sent Millais a £50 doctor bill.

While Lottie lay in state for about two weeks, thousands of local residents, dressed in their finest, came to stare at the decorously arrayed corpse in a display casket. This appears to have been culturally a women's liturgy of sorts, into which much can be read. Many men were undoubtedly dragged along, but it can be surmised that every woman of any sentiment in the San Diego region dressed in her finest, and made the pilgrimage to Lottie Bernard's casket—probably many more than once. Not only can this be taken as an unspoken signal of a fetal women's suffrage movement, but modern readers must remember the untold mortality rate among Victorians, especially among children. In the great wheel of history, whatever high mortality rates existed prior, and went unrecorded except in the parish registers of isolated hamlets, the Industrial Revolution jammed vast numbers of people together in cities whose size had not been seen in Europe since the decline of Rome, nearly fourteen centuries earlier. All these things transpired rather suddenly in the space of a century. In Britain, the Industrial Revolution (as we call it) began with the industrialization of manufacture in the late 1700s, a process that began half a century later in the United States, primarily in 1830s New England, and fortuitously creating the industrialized North that would vanquish the largely rural Southern Confederacy in the Civil War of the 1860s. The urbanization of Great Britain is mirrored in the growth of cities like New York, Boston, and Chicago, and in any case the culture that expressed itself in the mortuary room at Johnson & Company in 1892 was a direct consequence of all that. During the urbanization, British villages suffered. Politics was affected by issues of zoning, fencing, 'rotten boroughs' with empty voting constituencies in the House of Commons, and the like. London (and other U.K. cities) became famous for appalling smogs, caused by vast amounts of coal being burned, well into the 20th Century, when gasoline and oil burning contributed further and under different circumstances. London, Europe's largest city, and, like Imperial Rome two thousand years earlier, a vast melting pot of humanity flowing from all directions of the compass of an 'Empire on which the sun never sets," became a mass of suffering humanity coated with a thin cream of middle and upper class society. One of the Victorian era's chief romanticizers was Charles Dickens, who had risen from humble origins that he reflected in many of his works (he *was* David Copperfield and Oliver Twist, the poor little apprentices who suffered at the hands of cruel overseers and petty criminals). In some ways, it can be said that Dickens fairly invented the modern Christmas, with his collection of holiday stories to which he returned time and again, topped by "A Christmas Carol," in which poor little crippled Tim and the ugly Scrooge meet in battle upon the field of morality. Dickens, creator of Little Nell and, in his 1854 *Hard Times*, the indomitable little Sissy Jupe,[107] was the greatest of London's 19th Century investigative journalists.

Victorian sentimentalism:

As we begin to understand the Victorians a bit, we become less supercilious about their sentimentalism. On the one hand, we cannot help but marvel at the breathtaking hypocrisy of keeping her corpse lying in state, on display for tens of thousands to gawk at, then holding a solemn and magnificent High Church funeral with flowers, chorale, organ music, and many tears shed—and finally consigning her to a rude box on a donkey cart, rumbling alone and without a single mourner, to her final resting place in a barely marked grave on a lonely spot outside town. On the other hand, we have only to understand the brevity and cruelty of a life before modern medicine, when infant mortality was rampant, when death touched every doorway, to get some understanding of where that maudlin weepiness came from. It was a world still ruled mostly by medieval monarchs and medieval ideas, where the light of modernity had just begun to poke through the windows, but city streets were still covered in animal droppings. Most people lived a rough life on primitive farms, but city life was in many ways even more fearful with its crime and disease. In London, Charles Dickens was not only a novelist, but the premier crime reporter of his age—and we learn from him, and from the illustrations of Gustave Doré, the breathtaking depravity and poverty of urban life in the early industrial age. If the Victorian era strikes us as one of double standards and maudlin sentimentality, we must understand some of its fundamental, underlying stresses. For one thing, it is an era of tectonic change from rural to urban life on a scale not seen since perhaps Ancient Rome. In that sense it is almost a going backward while going forward. On the one hand, it can be seen as a return to the great but precarious city, with its urban mob for whom Vespasian built his Colosseum to keep them from overturning the state (as in recent memory a bloodthirsty rabble had plunged 1790s France into anarchy). On the other hand, one heard the siren songs of a renewed enlightenment based on science and mechanistic technology that promised hope for all problems. It was an age of utopian solutions and dystopian realities. The facts on the ground did not seem to gibe with the theories of prison reformers and other social engineers (including Karl Marx, whose footprint would extend through the horrors of the Paris Commune in the 1870s and into the dark maw of the middle twentieth century). It was an era when the final expansion of European culture pushed rough-hewn pioneers to the far western shores of Manifest Destiny, adapting to conditions as they found them, but bringing and preserving the trappings of the Eastern U.S. establishment, which itself was a Puritanized imitation of the parent British culture. In this split personality, the individual and social pretense was of a homogenously white, Anglo-Saxon Protestant culture, while the reality was of a mix of old Spanish, Native American, Black, Jewish, Mormon, Roman Catholic, and other identities that were overlaid by a ruling class that was largely WASP. Every California city of any size had a Chinatown, and many had a Japantown. The split personality of this society is evident in the fact that San Diego's city hall and police headquarters were within a stone's throw of one of the West Coast's most notorious dens of vice—the Stingaree. The double standard is probably best remembered into the twentieth century in a long tradition of movies whose story had few if any non-WASP characters in it. Actors had to Anglicize their names to suit the type. African-Americans in particular were nearly invisible and nonexistent in American cinema before Sidney Poitier came unexpectedly to dinner in 1967's *Guess Who's Coming To Dinner*. There might have been, by some estimates, a few hazy exceptions, as in 1939's *Gone With The Wind*. The American mythos playing on every movie and television screen, before the collapse of the Western genre in the 1970s, tended to portray the Homeric American hero as a purely WASP cowboy—when, in reality, the Old West was populated by a vivid blend of multi-cultural and multi-racial personas. Wyatt Earp, who lived in San Diego in the early 1890s as the Lottie Bernard drama unfolded, was married to a Jewish actress. Many of the cowboys trailing cattle as far north as Oregon were actually Mexican, and some of their terminology survives in the Klamath Marsh of central Oregon in words like *reata* (lariat) and *vaquero* (which survives in the English as 'buckaroo' for cowboy).

Aside from territorial social reproductive customs (e.g., a young woman can't travel alone, but must be in the company of a male relative or a female governess—a Victorian custom, whose analog is still active in many cultures around the world today, and which supports a double standard on sexuality. Life in the nineteenth century city was at least as dangerous as today's. There were few real police forces in the modern sense. San Diego organized its first rudimentary, uniformed police patrol just three years before the story related in this book. On June 1, 1889 lawman Joseph Coyne became San Diego's first metropolitan chief of police. The city would not have its first detective until 1907.[108]

Among the dangers of the age, the term 'shanghai' comes down to us today as a vague, quaint concept—but it was a reality in many port cities around the world. Many a farm boy stopped into a tavern for a drink in Portland, Oregon; or San Francisco; or San Diego—and woke up days later with a severe drug hangover, amid the salty sea air of a ship heading across the Pacific, and with a cracking whip and hard work to drive the cobwebs of his new reality away. Likewise, in this new urban hell, 'white slavers' often kidnapped women into 'white slavery,' and locked them up in dungeons where they became broken victims of drug addiction, disease, and prostitution. It was not only morally forbidden for the young woman to travel alone—it was dangerous. The way this entire schizoid reality could function was that there were 'things of which we do not speak.' The great Italian archeologist, Rodolfo Lanciani, father of modern Roman archeology, reported on a certain find from Ostia. He described this object from the ancient Classical world in terse wording as an object that "I have in possession, which I cannot name, but I know what it is." It was a sizeable ceramic dildo attached to a Priapus figure.

The Yellow Press exploited the events at the Hotel del Coronado with breathless reportage, fueled with both spoken and unspeakable insinuations, which made this story a national sensation in 1892. The fuel for that bonfire of titillation and sentimentality derives its fuel from the dark experiences and the morbid uncertainties of people who had all lost dearly loved ones—children, siblings, parents—to the cold and capricious cadaver claw of cruel and sudden death. It was the age of the 1889 Eiffel Tower, of Jules Verne's imaginative 1865 journey to the moon and back (*From The Earth To The Moon*), of an ocean-going vessel like 1863's *Euterpe* (now *The Star of India*, berthed in San Diego as a museum) that is a fully rigged sailing ship, yet also built of iron like the Eiffel Tower and 1851's Crystal Palace in London—a new Iron Age, an age of untold promise and excitement. And yet it was also an age of terrible mortality, straddling the dawn of modern surgical asepsis science (Listerism), safer food preservation techniques, and common sanitation. It is worth noting that, when President Abraham Lincoln was shot in 1865, and as he lay mortally wounded in a house across the street from Ford's theater, several prominent doctors rushed to the scene. The first of these used his unwashed fingers to probe directly into Lincoln's brain in an effort to locate the bullet. Another surgeon probed inside Lincoln's brain with a hooked metal probe. They managed to get the bullet out, but the doctors helped kill the patient. There lingered a cultural resistance among medical practitioners against Listerism (sterile environment and tools, and thorough hand washing), not to mention their ignorance of the brain as a delicate and complex organ. By cultural I mean a long-standing tradition—old as the ancient Roman republic in resisting Hellenic (Greek) baths, and surviving through the European medieval age—that bathing is somehow decadent and immoral. The Lincoln tragedy happened only a century and a half ago. Who knows what people 150 years from now will think of the current age. One thing is for sure, though—150 years from now, ghosts will be as much a part of the culture as they are now or were in Lottie A. Bernard's time.

women, two:

Throughout this story, we must follow two separate, interweaving threads—on one hand, the movements of Kate Morgan, the other hand, those of Lizzie Wyllie.

Traditionally, the story has been that a woman named Kate Morgan, aged about 26, of Hamburg, Iowa, checked into the Hotel del Coronado on Thursday, November 24, 1892. Her reason for coming to the Hotel Del, her reason for staying and the way she acted, and the cause of her death, are all central mysteries in a morass of loose ends, questions, and strange clues that seem to lead nowhere.

The official report of the Coroner's Inquest[109] certainly did not appear on or immediately after the day of the trial. The cover sheet of that document identifies her as both Lottie Anderson Bernard (the false name she used at the Hotel Del) and 'a.k.a.' (also known as) Kate Morgan. We know that this official transcript of the jury trial of November 30, 1892 was 'mislaid'[110] for a time (duration unknown) according to a written note in the official transcript by clerk W. W. Whitson. Since the name Kate Morgan did not enter public cognizance until at earliest December 6, 1892,[111] the jury's report could not have had this title sheet on it any sooner.

The jury, in fact, had no idea, since the name change happened after their brief, hasty deliberation. At the time of her death on November 28-29, she was thought to be who she had said she was: Lottie Anderson Bernard, wife or widow therefore of a putative Mr. Bernard who had not been seen, and who would never turn up—and sister of another figment, Dr. Anderson of Indianapolis, who also never showed up, because he never existed.

❧ ❦

Epilog:

The Big Picture

Of Sugar Barons and Pineapple Kings

The key to this entire story is John Spreckels, wealthy and brilliant heir of a great sugar fortune based on Hawai'ian plantations. Kate Morgan and her co-conspirators picked not only an impossible target, but the worst moment possible for their scheme. John Spreckels was a powerful man, no doubt surrounded by security apparatus and many functionaries—the Spreckels Machine, as I call it—or The Spreckels Corporation, as it was actually known.

As our glimpse of Kate Morgan's life has shown, she wove a net of conspiracy from city to city across the United States. The attempt to blackmail John Spreckels was probably her biggest gamble, and it failed horribly. She vanishes from the pages of history as completely as she briefly emerged in November and December 1892. Timing is everything, and her timing could not have been worse.

Two corporate giants were battling it out over the future of Hawai'i—Spreckels' pro-monarchy group, and Dole's annexation group. Both had insinuated themselves at the court of King David. Both owned land and power while the native Hawai'ians became disenfranchised. As we know, the Dole faction won after King David (a guest of John Spreckels at the Del for 1890 Christmas dinner in the Crown Room) died at the Palace Hotel in San Francisco as a guest of John's father Claus (January 20, 1891); and after the deposition of the last monarch, Queen Lili'uokalani almost exactly two years later (January 17, 1893). Claus Spreckels, who had made and lost fortunes before, shifted operations from Hawai'ian sugar cane to California sugar beets. The City of Spreckels near Monterey is named after him, and top sugar brands on the West Coast include Spreckels and C&H (California & Hawai'ian). These two brands are no longer owned by their founders.

Hawai'i had been ruled for nearly a thousand years by a feudal system of chiefs of varying ranks, headed by royal chiefs (*alibi*). By 1818, following a series of civil wars, a royal chief named Kamehameha had made himself the first king of a unified Hawai'i. The chiefs resented this new royal system, but it ironically saved Hawai'i for a long time from the fate of many other Pacific lands that became European colonies. The kings modernized Hawai'i. They brought in American and European entrepreneurs and innovators, who helped introduce a constitution, a bill of rights, and some land reform. Essentially, the Hawai'ians owned property communally, which hurt them after annexation under the U.S., when they could not legally and formally prove their ownership of land. In fact, under the monarchy, the trend was for elite native, European, and U.S. individuals to own most of the land, while the native people owned tiny plots or no land. There was a strong U.S. missionary influence, which tried to eradicate Hawai'i's native culture. The last king, David Kalakaua (ruled 1874-1891) made enemies among these dour Puritans (one of whom was Sanford Dole, who would become the first and only president of a short-lived Hawai'ian Republic, and whose cousin James would later build a fortune and become known as the Pineapple King). The first blow toward annexation came in 1887, when a combined force of U.S. Marines, the Honolulu Rifles, and other Dole-related interests forced the 'Bayonet Constitution' on King David. The king lost most of his administrative powers, while the average natives lost many fundamental rights (to vote; to own property; etc.), and ownership swung definitively to a small native and foreign elite. King David, the Merrie Monarch, had restored the hula and written poetry and created a Church of Hawai'i based on the Anglican Church—which enraged Calvinist U.S. missionaries soon instrumental in destroying Hawai'i's monarchy and independence. David died a few years later (1891) under odd circumstances, at the Palace Hotel in San Francisco, a guest of Claus Spreckels. Was he a victim of U.S. corporate interests coupled with dominant U.S. Protestant churches? This unpleasant question begs to be asked, though I am not the person to write that book. David Kalakaua, a relatively progressive thinker, had been the world's first monarch to circle the globe—on a goodwill tour to gain acceptance for his monarchy, and allied himself with Britain's Queen Victoria—after whom his niece Victoria Ka'iulani was named.

࿇ ࿇

If there was a truly beautiful and tragic woman who deserves mention, even if remotely and indirectly connected with our 1892 Hotel del Coronado mystery, it was the final player in the Hawai'ian Monarchy— Crown Princess Victoria Ka'iulani. Born in 1875, she was half European and half Hawai'ian. Her mother was the daughter of a Royal Chief related to the legendary King Kamehameha, founder of the first royal dynasty. Her father was a Scottish financier intimately involved in Hawai'ian affairs.

As Crown Princess, the teenage girl became the final royal in line for the throne. She was just 18 at the overthrow of the Queen in 1893 ended the Monarchy.

During her childhood, the Crown Princess lived in Honolulu. During her adolescence, still in Hawa'i, she became close friends with a sickly young man from Scotland, Robert Louis Stevenson, who was to pen some of the world's immortal literature.

Neither was destined for a long life. Stevenson retired to the South Sea Islands, where he died in the 1890s. The Crown Princess was named after Queen Victoria of England, and studied in England, traveled around the world seeking the restoration of her family's dynasty and her nation's independence. Her Hawai'ian name meant 'Highest Peak of Heaven.' She met with several U.S. Presidents and spoke with passion before Congress, all to no avail. It is said that the Crown Princess died of a broken heart—at age 24, in 1899, not long after learning of the death of her dear friend the author of *Kidnapped*, *Treasure Island*, and other enduring classics.

ॐ ☙

At the moment when Lottie A. Bernard checked into the Hotel del Coronado on Thanksgiving Day, 1892, John Spreckels was in Washington, D.C. lobbying with the President and Congress to avoid the overthrow of Hawai'i's monarchy. Claus Spreckels was at the Iolani Palace in Honolulu on Kissinger-style shuttle diplomacy to achieve the same end. All was in vain.

It goes without saying that Spreckels had a machinery of people of all levels, from ordinary night watchmen at his plants, to chief executives, bankers, security agents, newspaper executives and reporters, and armies of workers in his employ. The Spreckels Companies (owned by John and his brother Adolph) were the largest tax paying entity in San Diego County. In this book, when I referred to the Spreckels Machine, I am using a term I invented to describe a hypothetical organization that the mega-wealthy Spreckels family would logically have used or created. It would have been effective on behalf of John Spreckels, owner of the Hotel del Coronado—notably, against the likes of con artist and blackmailer Kate Morgan and her accomplices. The Pinkerton agency would have been quite experienced and adept in dealing with blackmail scenarios.

My theory is just that at the present—a theory. I have taken the facts as we know them, including the wealth of detail gathered by the Heritage Department from local resources including those at the San Diego Historical Society, the Coronado History Association, and the San Diego State University and San Diego City Libraries, and added my own research and thinking. I seem to be the first person to look at the tale of Lottie A. Bernard in its larger context, starting with ownership of the Hotel Del by John Spreckels, and extending to his concerns at the time—saving the Spreckels sugar plantations in Hawai'i—and interpreted the glaring beacons shining like lighthouses amid wreckage and mystery. I believe this interpretation stands the test of reasonableness.

If it is true that ghosts are restless shades of the dead, then is it not Lizzie Wyllie who troubles the quiet corridors of the Hotel del Coronado at night? Is it she who throws books off shelves and cries out for justice? Even her simple grave in a dusty corner of Mt. Hope Cemetery bears upon it the marker of the woman who betrayed and then impersonated her—Kate Morgan, who switched identities with the hapless, far prettier girl from Detroit, and made off with John Longfield. Does Lizzie make the curtains in Room 3327 room blow, though the windows are closed? Does she spin the tassels on the ceiling fan while guests lie innocently sleeping? Does she move their clothing and toiletry articles about, as so many people have reported? Did one just miss seeing her pale and vaporous form gliding down a dark and oddly twisting, narrow hallway, like a shadow or a shade?

Are there really ghosts? The mystery of Coronado begs the question. If ghosts are real, then the hundreds of reported incidents that continue to happen at the Hotel del Coronado would suggest there is an unquiet spirit who haunts the halls, seeking justice or at least attention. If there are not really such things as ghosts, this author feels that there is at least a kind of folk memory that survives and is passed along—in this case, the commemoration of a terrible event, the death of an innocent young woman, and her betrayal at the hands of the woman whose name is associated with the Beautiful Stranger's grave. In either case, our attention is called time and again to the plight of Lizzie Wyllie, the true victim of that night. Was it suicide, or was it murder? You judge. If a woman is betrayed and pushed beyond hope to commit suicide, who is to say it isn't murder?

As I said at the outset, there isn't a smoking gun. The many loose ends and frustrating dead ends tie together nicely and logically, once one starts with the fact that Spreckels owned the Hotel Del. The doomed 'Beautiful Stranger' registered there for a reason. Thereafter, many clues give the game away: The embroidered hankies in Room 302, bearing the names of Lizzie and Aunt Louisa; the moles on the left cheek; Katie Logan's stunning gaffe in Los Angeles (saying she was really Lizzie); the trunk in Los Angeles, containing artifacts of both Lizzie and Kate—these clues, and more, make a strong case for the solution I have laid out in this book. Equally convincing is the absolute certainty with which the poor girl's mother received the description of the corpse—certain beyond a doubt that it was her beloved daughter. Mrs. Elizabeth Wyllie, having learned the description of the woman found dead in Coronado, cried inconsolably and repeatedly cried: "It is my Lizzie, it is my Lizzie. Oh, what is to become of me now?"

The halls of the Hotel del Coronado are haunted as much by a loving mother's heart-rending cries, as by the ghost of a sweet and naïve young woman cut down in the flower of life. This very Victorian story leaves sentimental echoes in Coronado's balmy air, like a fading bloom of long-ago roses.

end

Appendix 1: Maps

These maps will help orient the reader to 1890s San Diego, as well as the travels of Kate Morgan and her accomplices.

The first map shows selected points on the transcontinental railroad system of the 1890s, particularly as it pertains to the movements of Tom and Kate Morgan, and their accomplices John Longfield and Elizabeth 'Lizzie' Wyllie.

The second map is an overview of greater San Diego, focusing on the harbor and bay, the Peninsula of San Diego (which includes the Silver Strand, South Island or Coronado incorporated 1891, the now-vanished Spanish Bight and isthmus connecting the two 'islands,' and North Island, which is now a U.S. Naval Air Station).

The third map is a general overview of San Diego, with two dots to orienting the reader to key points—the Hotel del Coronado (on Coronado Island), and the downtown San Diego area across the Bay.

The fourth and fifth maps are blown up from the inset in Map 3. The fourth map shows a closer view of Coronado and downtown San Diego. The fifth map shows the same detail, but with some of Lottie A. Bernard's key paths and wanderings highlighted.

Map 1: Transcontinental Rail System

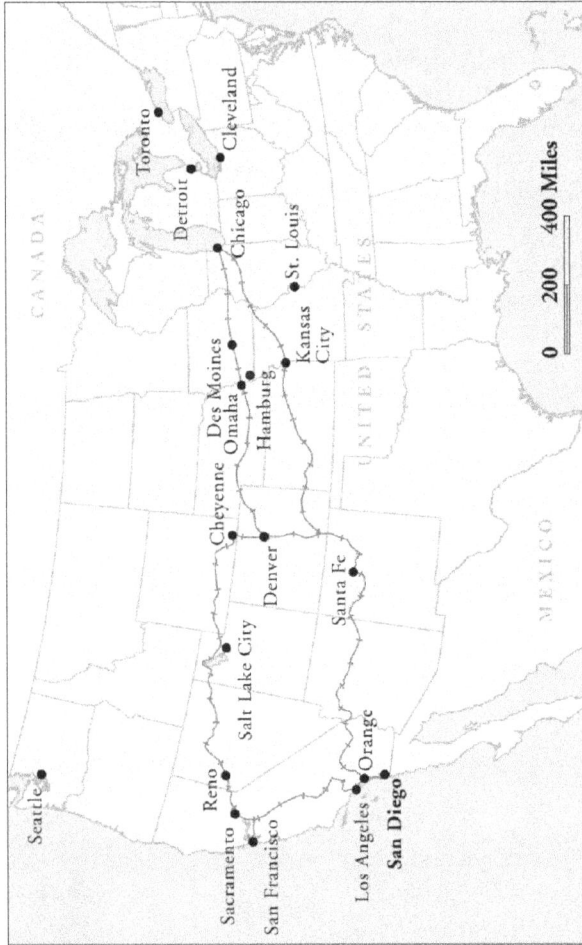

By 1892, railroads had been around for over half a century. The map above (Map 1) only shows a few selected stops and areas mentioned in this book. The country was so criss-crossed with rail lines that a complete map would look indecipherably black and veined. Here, we see selected cities mentioned in regard to Kate Morgan's mysterious aliases, or to her 'brother,' a 'doctor,' of such and such city, spanning much of the United States. Minneapolis, Indianapolis, and Detroit are among the cities she names in various schemes, as allegedly being where she or her doctor-brother are from.

There are several clusters of interest on this map.

San Francisco was the home base of the Spreckels family, and the place where the Hawai'ian king died in January 1891 as a guest of Claus Spreckels. Kate Morgan is known to have possessed business cards of several wealthy San Francisco families. Nearby are the towns of Hanford and Visalia (not shown), where Kate Morgan visited her uncle W. T. Farmer to obtain a job reference before traveling on to Los Angeles. In a hypothetical scenario, she might have altered the reference obtained from Farmer so it appears to be addressed to Katie Logan, the alter ego assumed by Lizzie Wyllie at several successive, brief temp jobs in Los Angeles area households.

Coronado (not shown) lies offshore from San Diego about a quarter mile on the San Diego Peninsula (described in subsequent maps). My theory, strongly supported by evidence, is that Kate trained Lizzie to impersonate a fictitious housekeeper (Katie Logan) to prepare her for her cameo role as the fictitious Lottie A. Bernard in Coronado the following month. In one of the most remarkable moments in this entire saga, the fictitious Katie Logan in L.A. blurts out to another housemaid that her real name is Lizzie, then quickly corrects herself and gets even her phony name wrong, saying that she goes by Kittie or Katie, since she prefers that name. A number of odd things and odd moments in the saga helped convince me of my version. For example, witnesses reported that the fictitious Lottie A. Bernard (Lizzie Wyllie) arrived in San Diego and went directly to the Hotel Brewster downtown—ostensibly to ask about her 'brother, Doctor Anderson, and his wife' (John Longfield and Kate Morgan). That is yet another indicator of her accomplices in an obvious plot.

The Iowa/Nebraska area is significant. The southwest corner of the former (Hamburg, Fremont, etc.) was home to both Kate Farmer (Morgan) and Tom Morgan. Tom settled in south-central Nebraska after the Lottie A. Bernard affair, remarried, and lived a long and prosperous life as a church deacon, postal worker, constable, and other responsible jobs. While Lottie A. Bernard was at the Hotel del Coronado, Kate Morgan sent or accompanied John Longfield, or Tom Morgan, or both, to Hamburg to induce a bank manager to hold $25 on credit in case the woman in faraway Coronado needed it.

Finally, we have a cluster of cities around the Great Lakes. Lizzie and John Longfield were from Detroit (a city mentioned in connection with one of Kate Morgan's aliases, so it is possible she and Tom met Lizzie and John there as this novel suggests. Grand Rapids was the home of Lizzie's sister Louisa, where Lizzie fled upon discovering she was (once again) pregnant out of wedlock, and no doubt having a spat with her mother; most likely the source of the monogrammed handkerchiefs mentioned in the coroner's inquest. Cleveland was where John Longfield strangely and implausibly turns up later, acting as an intermediary between Lizzie—who (he claims, implausibly) is alive and well in Toronto and will never again contact (oh, because she is dead?) her loving mother and sister—and Mrs. Longfield, who (implausibly) is acting as a somewhat dim interlocutor between the Wyllies and John Longfield.

Toronto, finally, is the alleged place where Lizzie has run off and will never again contact her loving family. That is one of the most implausible elements in the entire fabricated story I believe Kate Morgan and Longfield pulled off to cover their tracks. In my scenario, Lizzie was the housemaid missing from Los Angeles and acting as Lottie A. Bernard in Coronado. It is not a much farther stretch to suppose that Kate Morgan and John Longfield had become lovers by now, and that she was orchestrating a rather lame plot (that worked, in any case, since nobody seems to have questioned it) to cover her escape to Toronto under the guise of being Lizzie Wyllie. Kate Morgan, the woman of so many aliases, left her identity on the back steps of the Hotel del Coronado, stealing the dead woman's name and identity, as well as her lover, and made off for distant parts, while Tom Morgan (if that was him at all, by Kate's side, and not some unnamed other male lover) returned to Nebraska and started a long new life. What became of John Longfield and Kate Morgan I can only guess; maybe another researcher will find the answer. She probably dumped him and moved on again to some new frontier—her own identity now forever unusable.

Map 2: San Diego and Peninsula with Coronado

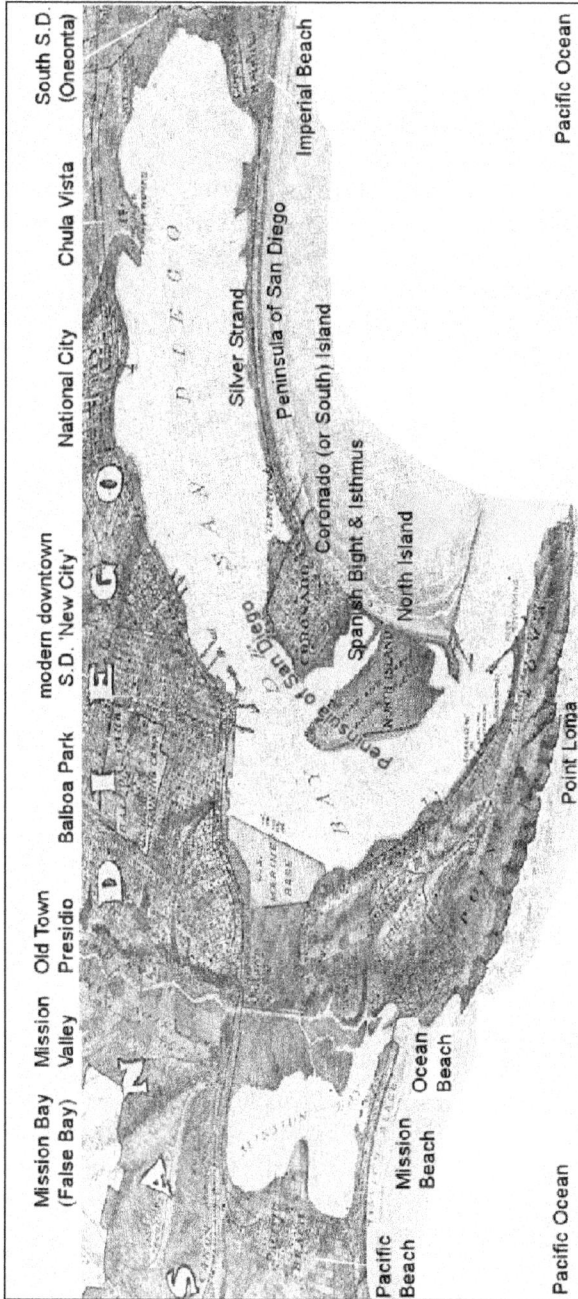

This antique aerial view adds another perspective on the two cities. San Diego Bay is the main body of water (shown on map). It is about 12 mi/19 km long, 1 mi/1.6 km–3 mi/4.8 km wide, and bordered by the Cities of Coronado, San Diego, National City, modern Chula Vista, and Imperial Beach. San Diego Harbor is the waterfront that stretches along San Diego's downtown.

Point Loma, at its tip, was where, in 1542, the first Spanish ships arrived under Juan Cabrillo, for whom the national park at the tip of Point Loma is named. He named the settlement San Miguel, but the name was changed to San Diego in 1602, when Sebastián Vizcaíno arrived with the next expedition. Point Loma was the setting of the Theosophical Society— which in Chapter 10 of my novel Lethal Journey I have L. Frank Baum visiting in 1892, while also meeting Lottie A. Bernard (poor Lizzie) at the Hotel del Coronado.

* * * *

The San Diego River flows westward, from the mountains and deserts, through Mission Valley, and to the sea. At one time, the river emptied into False Bay (today's Mission Bay), which may have seemed like a good harbor at first glance, but proved shallow and useless for ocean-going ships. By contrast, San Diego Bay is one of the finest natural harbors on the West Coast. The San Diego River changed course in recent centuries, and emptied into San Diego Bay. Because of silting and other concerns, the city diverted it along a channel, through Mission Bay, into the sea.

The Mission (California's first, San Diego de Alcalá) was founded by Spanish Franciscan friars in 1769, led by Father Junipero Serra. The original mission was located defensively near the Presidio (garrison) near the mouth of Mission Valley, because the native population were hostile to the invading Spaniards. Later, the Spaniards moved the mission further east along the San Diego River, to what became Grantville after the Civil War of 1861-65. Grantville, still a community of San Diego today, was a small town created as a settlement for Civil War veterans. It lay isolated in the swampy marshes around the San Diego River, amid dairy farms that covered a rural and sparsely populated Mission Valley until the latter half of the 20th Century.

The explorer Richard Henry Dana, in 1836 during the Mexican period (1821-1848), in his journal *Two Years Before The Mast*, reported that San Diego contained only the Presidio, the Mission, a small Spanish settlement known today as Old Town, and—on the beach—a shack for storing tanned hides. The mission fell into ruin and disuse, but was given to a Catholic Church organization after the Civil War by President Lincoln. It has been restored and remains under archeological excavation. Today it is an active

Catholic church and basilica, and claims to be the oldest functioning church in California.

Old Town, today mainly a tourist destination, was the original Spanish, later Mexican, settlement in the safe shadow of the Presidio. This garrison, home of the first Spanish imperial governor of Alta California, has been restored as Presidio Park, overlooking the mouth of Mission Valley from a cliff on the south face of the valley entrance and river channel.

The New City, as opposed to the Old Town, came about with the arrival of a Connecticut Yankee named Alonzo Horton. He, moving in from San Francisco, saw that the great harbor was booming with ships, yet the population was centered miles inland to the north around Old Town. He bought 960 acres of barren land near the waterfront, and created what is today downtown San Diego. By then, Old Town had fallen into disuse, and hardly anyone lived there anymore. It was, for quite a time, 'out of town' as San Diego became the New City.

In the New City, Lottie A. Bernard arrived by train at the old Santa Fe depot at Kettner and D, now Broadway or West Broadway. She walked to the Brewster Hotel some blocks east, at 4th and C to ask about her two accomplices (and instead received the 'terrible medicines' mentioned by Dr. Mertzmann to induce a spontaneous abortion). She then headed back west to the ferry landing and off to Coronado to stay at the Hotel Del.

The New City is where Lottie later bought the gun with which she shot herself. The New City was where Wyatt Earp owned four gambling casinos, while he also ran horses at the Del Mar track some miles north. The New City also contained the notorious Stingaree red light district, and a small Chinatown.

Both National City and Chula Vista were newly incorporated during the late 1800s. Otay is a region in the unincorporated areas of San Diego County. South San Diego is part of the City of San Diego, also known as San Ysidro. However, the land area that meets the Silver Strand, the narrow strip of land going to Coronado, is the City of Imperial Beach (not shown on this map). The city now known as Chula Vista was a vast, privately owned preserve dedicated to the health craze of the time, known as Oneonta.

* * * *

Map 2, at lower center, shows Point Loma. This peninsula, which juts southward from the Ocean Beach and Loma Portal areas, shields the harbor entrance of San Diego Bay. By 'bay,' we mean the entire body of water enclosed within Point Loma and the Peninsula of San Diego, from Imperial Beach on the Mexican border to the south, as far north as the inner shores of Point Loma.

Not shown on the map is Ballast Point, so named because sailing vessels used to stop there and load rocks for ballast. That lies along the inner shore of Point Loma, just as you enter the harbor. Also not clearly labeled, but clearly shown, is a light-colored area of low-lying land, which was at various times property of the U.S. Army and the U.S. Marine Corps. It is now the general location of Lindbergh Field, San Diego's International Airport. This is one of the world's oldest commercial airfields, and one of the few major airports in the world that is practically located downtown.

Two modern features that did not exist in Lottie A. Bernard's time are Shelter Island and Harbor Island, both created largely from dredging operations along the bay near the airport. These dredging operations, conducted by both private and Navy operations, expanded the harbor. The Navy finished the last of these operations by 1945, eliminating the small bay, or bight, between North and South Islands.

One important feature not shown here, because it did not yet exist, is the Coronado Bay Bridge, emblematic of San Diego. The Bridge, completed 1969 and 2.2 miles long, rises nearly 300 feet above the water at its highest point. It rises from 4th Street in Coronado heading southeast, and curves around to the mainland. From the San Diego side it rises westward, starting at U.S. Interstate 5 in the Barrio Logan neighborhood.

It is useful to understand the Peninsula of San Diego, in reference to the surroundings in which Lottie A. Bernard and her contemporaries moved in the 1890s. This major geographical feature shapes San Diego's great natural harbor. It helps define San Diego, yet is not well understood even by many residents. Think of the Bay as being sheltered by two arms—one the Peninsula of San Diego which comes north, and Point Loma, a smaller peninsula that juts southward and overlaps the Peninsula of San Diego at North Island, as shown on the map. The best vantage point to see the entire city and bay is from atop Cabrillo Point, a national park situated high up on the outermost tip of Point Loma.

Originally, the peninsula consisted of the following main elements:

- **North Island** was originally an empty sand flat used for hunting jack rabbits, North Island has long been home of U. S. Naval Air Station North Island. Since about 1911, it has always been associated with military aviation—Army, Marine Corps, and, since 1917, Navy. The twin concrete hangars were featured in the 1935 James Cagney movie about U.S. Marine Corps aviation, *Devil Dogs of the Air*. Congress named North Island "the birthplace of naval aviation" in 1963. In 1927, Charles Lindbergh started from North Island on his famous flight across the U.S, across the Atlantic, and to Paris.

- **Spanish Bight**, a body of water that disappeared by 1945 as it was filled in by harbor dredging operations, especially by the U.S. Navy during World War II. A bight is what geographers call a smaller bay inside a larger bay. The strip of land joining North Island and South Island is called an isthmus. Though Spanish Bight is gone, a trace of its northern lip perhaps remains in that the mooring berths of the aircraft carriers *U.S.S. Reagan* and *U.S.S. Nimitz* are sharply angled in relation to one another, suggesting the northern lip of the vanished bight mouth. The isthmus that connected North and South Islands has vanished into the landmass of the greater peninsula.

- **Coronado Island**, or South Island. Elisha Babcock and Hampton Story used to go fishing in the bay, or come to the islands to hunt jackrabbits. Both islands (neither technically an island, but parts of a peninsula) were barren tracts overrun with brush and jackrabbits. Babcock had the soaring vision to buy the peninsula, develop it into a city, and use the sale of lots to finance a world-famous resort hotel. From that inspiration to the finished Hotel Del, and the developed community, took about four or five years (1884-1888). By 1889, San Diego was bust, Spreckels had bought out Story, and Babcock was sliding toward his ultimate bankruptcy. By 1892, Spreckels was the sole owner of the Del, and of most of the rest of Coronado and San Diego. The City of Coronado was incorporated 1891. Babcock had installed docks, ferry service, trolleys, and many other modern amenities.

- The **Silver Strand**, a long, thin strip of land stretching eight miles from Coronado in the north to Imperial Beach in the south. Became the home of the famous Tent City during the health craze starting around 1900 and lasting roughly until the Depression Era 1930s. Had a light rail system running circa 1900. Note: Coronado (incorporated as a city on South Island in 1991) had its own trolley that Lizzie rode several times—including the day she bought her gun in San Diego, with which she committed suicide at the Hotel Del.

In modern times, Spanish Bight is gone. North Island and South Island have fused into one landmass, containing North Island Naval Air Station at the northern end, and the City of Coronado at the southern end. From the City of Coronado, on Fourth Street, the soaring curve of the Coronado Bay Bridge connects the peninsula to the mainland in the City of San Diego. The Silver Strand remains, connecting Coronado with Imperial Beach. After the turn of the 20th Century (when Lottie A. Bernard lay buried and forgotten), the strand became home to the famous Tent City, part of the national health craze of the time.

Map 3: San Diego Overview

Map 3 is an overview of San Diego around 1890 or 1900, with selected details shown. The inset area refers to the next two maps.

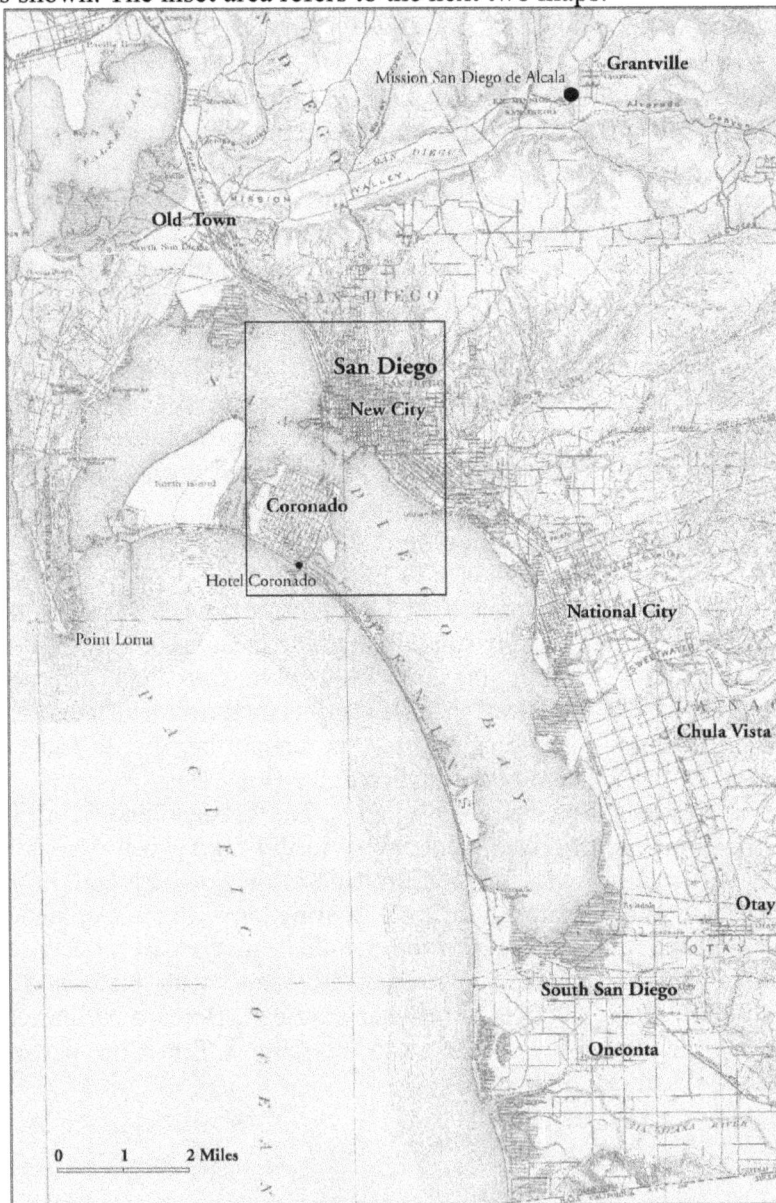

This inset focuses primarily on downtown San Diego (New City) and the City of Coronado around the time of Kate Morgan.

Coronado (2007 population 26,600) was part of the barren Peninsula of San Diego purchased 1884 by a consortium led by Elisha Babcock. Babcock and his partners developed South Island, or Coronado Island, and built the Hotel del Coronado. The grand resort was opened for business in February 1888. It is shown as the black dot on the southern beach of Coronado in Map 3, and this is where Lottie A. Bernard spent her few remaining days. The crown jewel of Coronado, the Hotel del Coronado, is where the main action of this true story takes place. Lottie A. Bernard was found shot to death on the back steps toward Ocean Boulevard on the morning of November 29, 1892.

Coronado, as it is laid out today, follows much the same street layout created by Babcock and his engineers. In the center of the island is Spreckels Park, named after the man who practically owned Coronado and San Diego for at least a generation. Opposite the Hotel Del, across Orange Avenue, today is the Glorietta Bay Inn—built after 1906 as the private mansion of John Spreckels. After the terrible earthquake in San Francisco, Spreckels moved with his wife and children to Coronado. At the corner of Orange Avenue and Adella Avenue, a block away, stands the Hotel El Cordoba, long ago the mansion of Elisha Babcock, chief builder and briefly owner of the Hotel del Coronado until ousted by Spreckels during the financial collapse in San Diego, starting 1889. We see this a little better in Maps 4 and 5.

Map 4: San Diego and Coronado (3 Inset—Detail)

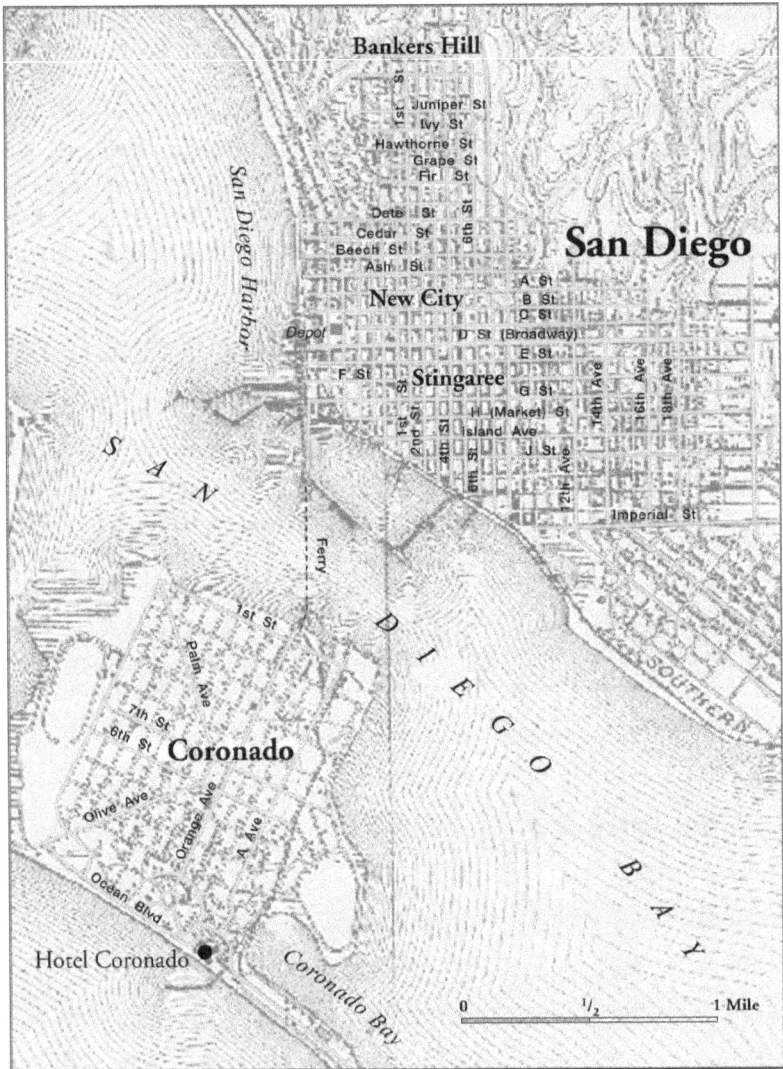

Map 5: San Diego and Coronado (Inset, Detail 2)

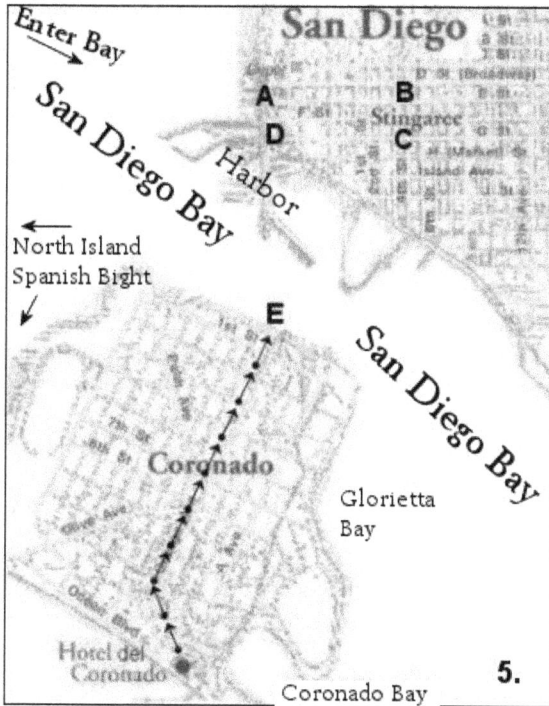

San Diego (2007 population 1.3 million): The New City is logically laid out (except that frequent deep canyons cause modern motorists to go bonkers as streets stop abruptly and start again across a chasm).

The main streets running east-west are lettered. This is important to understand in following Lottie A. Bernard's journey. In Map 2, notice Balboa Park and downtown. The dividing line (not shown) is at Ash Street, which runs east-west along the base of this enormous urban park (one of the world's largest, containing among other things the San Diego Zoo). Parallel to Ash Street, along its south side, is A Street. Beginning with Ash Street, the streets north of Ash are alphabetically named after trees (Ash, Beech, Cedar, Elm, etc.). The streets running east-west south of A Street are alphabetic (A, B, C, D, E, F, G, and a few more). In Lottie's time, today's Broadway was D Street. Also, her H Street is our modern Market Street. The notorious red light district, or Stingaree, occupied an area of some eight or ten city blocks (opinions vary) but conformed generally to today's commercially attractive and busy tourist area, the Gaslamp District. That's roughly from today's Petco Park baseball stadium north to Broadway (Lottie's D Street), and from as far west as parts of the waterfront to as far east as around Sixth or Seventh Avenues.

Running north and south, for most of the city, are numbered streets, except at the harbor front. From the water, we have Harbor Drive, Pacific Highway, Kettner Boulevard, and then these streets: India, Columbia, State, Union, and Front. From there, the north-south streets are in a fairly orderly grid, running from First into the double digits. All the numbered streets were streets in Lottie's time. With development, the first twelve streets became avenues. Where Interstate-5 is today was 18th Street in Lottie's time.

In Lottie A. Bernard's time, Wyatt Earp presided over four major gambling saloons in the Stingaree (sprawling between First and Fifth Streets, and Market and K). Lottie (Kate Morgan or Lizzie Wyllie, q.v.) trudged a relatively small area, from the railway terminal on Kettner to the Hotel Brewster, from the ferry landing to buy her gun on Fifth Street. In fact, her final journey was from the undertakers on Fifth Street (today's Fifth Avenue) to Mt. Hope Cemetery on Market Street. She is buried at Mt. Hope Cemetery, which was then outside of town, in the 3700 block of Market Street (then H Street).

Looking at Map 5 in particular, Point A indicates the area around the Santa Fe Depot (train station) where Lottie arrived in San Diego on Thanksgiving Day 1892. It was where her three trunks were kept, which she was never able to retrieve.

When she first arrived, she walked up D Street (today's Broadway) to Point B, the Hotel Brewster on 4th and D (my theory: to retrieve her abortion medicine, left there by Kate and John).

I have indicated as Point D the general area of the ferry landing(s) around G Street, where she most likely took the ferry back and forth between Coronado and San Diego. Her landing on Coronado was not the modern ferry landing, but Point E, where Centennial Park is today—some of the concrete footings of the dock are still visible. The modern ferry landing is a short walk from there.

Author 2008 photo 300ft above the Coronado Bay Bridge—see the modern San Diego waterfront at right. At the foot of the tallest buildings, center, is the Navy Pier area, within a block of the old Grand Union Depot, which was replaced 1914 by the Santa Fe Terminal. At left is the area of modern and (demolished) 19th century ferry landings. The 1892 ferry landing that Lottie A. Bernard used is gone, replaced by Centennial Park, but traces of the concrete dock remain. The 1890s ferries were steel ships, capable of loading horses and wagons, and bigger than today's ferry.)

Lizzie traveled on Orange Avenue on a trolley, which ran down the center where today we see green grass, flowers, and palm trees. At first, when the trolley tracks were removed in the early 1900s, they were replaced by a long strip of fragrant orange trees. However, the perpetual bane of Coronado Island was the jack rabbit, in limitless multitudes, who loved oranges. To rid the area of jack rabbits, it is said, the city decided to plant grass and palm trees instead.

Selected Reading:

Beautiful Stranger: The Ghost of Kate Morgan and the Hotel del Coronado
by Heritage Department, Hotel del Coronado
(Hotel del Coronado, 2002, 2005, etc.)

San Diego: California's Cornerstone
by Engstrand, Iris (Ph.D.):
(Sunbelt, 1980)

San Diego's Gaslamp Quarter
by The San Diego Gaslamp Quarter Association & The San Diego Historical Society:
(Arcadia, 2003)

The Story of New San Diego and of its Founder, Alonzo E. Horton
by McPhail, Elizabeth C.:
(San Diego Historical Society, 1979)

Website of the San Diego History Center:
http://www.sandiegohistory.org/

Website of the Coronado Historical Association:
http://coronadohistory.org/

Website of the San Diego Police Historical Association
http://www.sdpolicemuseum.com/

Notes:

1. Note about Wikipedia: The 'Kate Morgan' entry at Wikipedia perpetuates the erroneous myth that the dead woman found at the Hotel del Coronado was Kate Morgan. I have independently concluded, without reference to any of this online material, that Tom Morgan appears not to have been involved in the crime. I have no comment on the Iowa background—interesting to some, but it has no direct bearing on the overall outcome of my research. The dead woman was not Kate Morgan, but Elizabeth 'Lizzie' Wyllie—as I have minutely and accurately detailed in this book.

2. The Legend of Kate Morgan: The Search for the Ghost of the Hotel del Coronado. By Alan M. May (ELK Publishing 1987, 1991) This book created a great deal of new misinformation, on top of the already baffling disinformation resulting from the 1892 cover-up of what really happened. Mr. May's book rekindled interest in the long-dormant story, which had been doctored into incomprehensibility by Spreckels' agents in 1892, and further suppressed by the hotel management over many decades. It should be noted that the Spreckels family owned the Hotel del Coronado until around 1948, after which time it was owned by various unrelated individuals or corporations. The Heritage Department appears to have published its excellent book Beautiful Stranger: The Ghost of Kate Morgan and the Hotel del Coronado in 2001 to counteract the misinformation of Alan May's sensational 1987 book. Mr. May's book caused local authorities to briefly reopen the investigation of 1892, but they quickly closed it, citing a lack of substantive new evidence in Mr. May's book. Mr. May died before actual publication in 1987. Mr. May claimed, among other things, to be descended from Kate Morgan (utterly unlikely), and that he, Alan May, regularly had dinner with the ghost in her former room at the Hotel del Coronado. The latter item, alone, should be enough to help the critical thinker and sensible reader draw their own conclusions.

3. The only two books I would recommend for reading about this true crime story are Beautiful Stranger: The Ghost of Kate Morgan and the Hotel del Coronado (official publication by the HdC Heritage Department) and Dead Move: Kate Morgan and the Haunting Mystery of Coronado (my analysis of the case, which you are reading, first published in 2008). While the hotel's otherwise excellent book continues to support the misleading idea that Kate Morgan was the victim, my book shows the victim was Lizzie Wyllie, and Kate Morgan was her mentor, accomplice, and ultimately worst betrayer.

About Clocktower Books:

Internet and Digital Publishing Pioneer Since 1996

Clocktower Books is a recognized publisher of the Internatial Thriller Writers (ITW), and John T. Cullen is an Active Member of ITW.

Clocktower Books has been noted by many resources, especially in the early days of the World Wide Web. These include the Wayback Machine, Encyclopedia Britannica Online in a 1998 article about Clocktower Fiction, the Encyclopedia of Science Fiction (for our acclaimed online magazine Deep Outside/Far Sector SFFH which ran for a decade 1998-2007); and more.

Clocktower Books has published books and shorter works by over one hundred authors, including several still on the roster in 2017. Among them, listed here in random order, are Renée B. Horowitz, Dennis Latham, Robin Marchesi, Deborah Cannon, and more.

John T. Cullen, publisher of Clocktower Books, has released over forty books, stories, articles, and more (fiction, nonfiction, poetry) under the names John T. Cullen, John Argo (his 1996 name for speculative fiction), and Jean-Thomas Cullen (his actual birth name of European origin).

We Made History

Lots More Where These Came From...

Please visit the website of Clocktower Books for a full listing of our exciting fiction and nonfiction books, articles, and short works by a variety of talented authors.

www.clocktowerbooks.com

Also visit the Museum Site of Clocktower Books for a great deal of fascinating history detailing the author's and publisher's pioneering presence on the Internet since early 1996.

www.museum.fyi

The author's personal website, part of a webplex of more than two dozen linked websites, is

www.johntcullen.com

Appendix 2: Prefaces (Moved to Rear)

As indicated earlier in the Brief Foreword (2020 Edition), I found the growing number of prefaces over the years to start looking cluttered, so I moved them to the rear (in this Appendix) so readers can quickly access the original 2008/2009 Prolog and get into the story. The following information is a bit chatty, perhaps, but contains some of the growing amount of incredible background information. It's a story that starts with a rather daring through humdrum local crime (blackmail) and quickly expands within context to a global affair in 1892.

Preface to the 2020 Edition of Dead Move

As I go to press with the 2020 Edition, I wish to affirm that my conclusions of the previous dozen years have only confirmed themselves over time and through continuing reflection. And I offer some cautions.

The mystery of Coronado in 1892 is worthy of a real investigation. We have a famous ghost legend, created from a true crime with national and international repercussions stretching from San Diego to Washington, D.C., from San Francisco to Honolulu, Hawai'i, and to London, U.K. Among the peripheral figures that come to light are U.S. President Benjamin Harrison, Hawai'ian Queen Lili'uokalani and her beautiful, doomed young Crown Princess Victoria Ka'iulani (the other tragic woman in this saga, besides Lizzie Wyllie), and in fact also Queen Victoria, who was the namesake and godmother of the Crown Princess.

My interest in this case began as I worked in a fun, part-time position at the Hotel Del 2006 to 2008 as a shuttle driver. My wife engineered for me to get me out of the house: a retired writer, journalist, and editor pounding a keyboard night and day, and you can imagine how my wife felt about that. She hooked me up with the Transportation Department through her personal/professional nursing channels and connections. It turned out to be one of the most enjoyable jobs I have ever held.

In order to answer the many questions asked by hotel guests on the way from the airport to the hotel (ten miles), we were asked by the hotel to learn as much about their history and the local (Coronado, San Diego) history as possible. That was like offering sugary donuts to someone with a sweet tooth, since I earned several college degrees spread over History,

Literature, Comparative Lit, Classics, and Modern Languages; plus a Master's in Business Administration from Boston University, earned while serving honorably with the U.S. Army many years earlier in what was then the Federal Republic of Germany. I fell in love with the story, as told in the hotel's own official Heritage Department book *Beautiful Stranger*. I found that book to be attractive and well-researched, but muddled in its (lack of) conclusions. Rather, I found the lack of firm conclusions admirable in a guarded sort of scholarly way, but also found some serious missing pieces that would, of necessity, open the door to serious further questions that nobody had apparently sought to ask. My resolve was not to actually solve the more than a century old cold case, although I think that is what I have done. My resolve was to use the great information in the hotel's book to see what conclusions I might arrive at. I ended up doing a lot of research on my own, particularly using the newly available Internet resources, in a guarded sense, knowing how much misinformation and disinformation is out there. This brings me to a cautionary note.

It is worthy of a sad comment that apparently, a subject of this type stirs up quite a number of trolls and saboteurs who, for unfathomable reasons, seek to muddy the waters, confuse the issues, and just as often spread falsehoods. In a moment, I will cite two or three examples of the mischief I want to warn readers about. Don't get sucked in by the crazies and crooks. I have outlined a logical, fact-based, history-driven narrative that I believe is the best and only plausible explanation for the mystery that occurred at the Hotel del Coronado in November 1892.

The only reason I go into the following detail is to caution readers: don't let opportunists and falsifiers with agendas lead you astray. Among those whose ire I aroused by publishing this material has been a charlatan who claims to be channeling Kate Morgan's ghost (total nonsense) and other famous, deceased women for a hefty fee. At least two crazies have published spurious books on the subject, claiming to be descendants of either Tom Morgan or of Kate Morgan, which have (to be charitable) added very little to an honest, scholarly understanding of these events.

Take my word for it. I began this investigation in total innocence and naïveté, and came to realize that there are a number of dishonest souls out there who either want to make money on a notorious true crime (and resulting famous ghost legend) like this, or simply sabotage an honest, clean investigation for no real reason.

I state my case clearly and honestly, and can defend every position I have taken on the myriad puzzle pieces that go into this complex case—for the most part, using the information contained in the Hotel Del Coronado's official (and well researched but ambivalently-concluded) book. To that point: the hotel's handling of the 1892 true crime was for a long time to avoid discussing it. A very bad book published in the 1980s, filled with absurdities (e.g., having dinner with the alleged ghost in her long-ago room every night) briefly stirred up popular discussion, and spread all sorts of false stories (that Tom Morgan was not only a gambler on trains, not true; but that he murdered people; no evidence for any such fantasies). As a result, it is not surprising in the chain of events to see the Hotel Del sponsor an official history (*Beautiful Stranger*) in the early 2000s, which is both entertaining and informative, but draws no conclusions about who the dead person was. And the hotel's official historian has gone on record stating that they don't ever want the case solved, because they are so enamored of the ghost legend. In short, the hotel's official book is marvelously researched and filled with true historical information, but then becomes little more than an entertaining promo for the ghost legend. I was not interested in the ghost legend, but in the true crime. My position on the ghost story is that I remain neutral: if you don't believe in ghosts, I offer a rousing true history, true crime tale. If you do want to believe in the famous ghost legend, then my exposé in Dead Move will tell you how she became a ghost... that is Lizzie Wyllie, not the dark and sociopathic grifter Kate Morgan who caused all the mayhem and then vanished into history, leaving her accomplices in the lurch: John Longfield fleeing back to Detroit to his wife and children; poor Lizzie dead on the hotel's rear steps.

I would still call the 1892 true crime a cold case that has never really been solved; dismissed, yes; solved, no.

Consider, for example, that this is likely the only violent death we'll ever hear about that results in a death certificate with two different names on it, without explanation.

Consider, also, that the court transcripts vanished for a number of days or weeks, meaning the chain of custody was broken, and reappeared mysteriously (probably after the Spreckels Machine had time to doctor what was in the official records).

Consider that the records themselves originated in a rushed, sham coroner's jury allowed only half a day's trial time, a day or so after the body was found, leaving zero time for investigation.

Consider that the leading physician in San Diego, Dr. Mertzman, was not allowed to do an autopsy but only a brief, cursory examination of the body; even at that, Dr. Mertzman's three chief observations made to the jury are stunning: she was pregnant; she was taking "terrible medicines" to induce an abortion; and she had given birth at least once before. There are easily deducible reasons for all this. The outcome was a coverup to protect John Spreckels, owner of the Hotel Del, from financial and personal ruin in a very prudish, unforgiving Victorian society.

Even more amazingly, the context and circumstances for this brief crime event at the Hotel Del reach literally around the globe. Spreckels was in Washington, D.C. negotiating for the future of his father's sugar plantations in Hawai'i. His father, Claus Spreckels, was doing desperate, last-minute shuttle diplomacy (as this was to become known during Henry Kissinger's years as Secretary of State during the Nixon and Ford administrations nearly a century later) between his home base in San Francisco and his operating base in Honolulu, primarily at the royal Iolani Palace of Queen Lili'uokalani... who was to be overthrown by the Dole interests a few weeks later. Hawai'i, a sovereign nation recognized around the world, thus became a phony republic under Dole for a short time, after which it was handed over to U.S. interests as a 'territory,' meaning the formerly free citizens of Hawai'i no longer enjoyed full democratic representation until statehood was declared in 1959. This is a massive global crime for which the U.S. Government, in a bi-partisan move on the hundredth anniversary of the overthrow, officially apologized to the people of Hawai'i; this from Democratic President Bill Clinton and the Republican-controlled Congress. United States Public Law 103-150, informally known as the Apology Resolution, is a Joint Resolution of the U.S. Congress adopted in 1993 that "acknowledges that the overthrow of the Kingdom of Hawaii occurred with the active participation of agents and citizens of the United States and further acknowledges that the Native Hawaiian people never directly relinquished to the United States their claims to their inherent sovereignty as a people over their national lands..."

* * *

As mentioned in a previous preface, I wrote the nonfiction *Dead Move* according to strict, objective scholarship. When I was persuaded to write a noir, gaslamp period novel (*Lethal Journey*), I removed the original dramatization from Dead Move and fashioned as dramatic a novel as I could. My goal was to adhere as closely as possible to the research in *Dead Move*, with one major exception. There is no evidence that Tom Morgan, husband of grifter Kate Morgan, ever set foot in San Diego. He never gambled on trains, nor did he murder people as some of the more absurd stories about the case have claimed. However, with the mission in mind of creating the most dramatic possible novel, I included a fictional Tom Morgan in *Lethal Journey* as a key villain.

As a lesser liberty I took in the novel, though not the nonfiction book: I wrote the novel *Lethal Journey* in 2008, closely based on my extensive research reflected in the nonfiction, scholarly analysis (*Dead Move*), as a dramatization and easy, entertaining way to grasp the highlights of a very complex investigation. In the novel, I took a few liberties (clearly and honestly stated) like, in the spirit of an informed guess or thought experiment, I would assume that the Beautiful Stranger had a powerful reason for signing in at the Hotel del Coronado under the false name "Lottie A. Bernard." My best guess was that, since my theory is that the case was an attempt at blackmailing the owner of the Hotel Del at the time (John Spreckels, one of the wealthiest men in the United States), the trio of blackmailers would want to send a message to Spreckels. Spreckels was, at that moment, in the White House in Washington, D.C., working feverishly with President Benjamin Harrison to avert the overthrow of the legitimate government of Hawai'i by a U.S. corporate gang of rivals led by the so-called Pineapple King, Sanford Dole.

To be clear: neither the Spreckels nor the Dole interests were above blame; and President Harrison, a Republican, was interested in expanding the United States' growing reach around the world.

As the plot at the Hotel Del unfolded during Thanksgiving week 1892, John Spreckels (wealthy son of so-called Sugar Baron Claus Spreckels) could not afford a breath of scandal. This was during Victorian times, remember, and even a hint of an extra-marital affair by John Spreckels with one of the billionaire family's many house maids would almost certainly wipe out U.S. support for the Spreckels faction, resulting in a disaster for Spreckels' Hawai'ian sugar empire. In *Dead Move*, after much deliberation, I have concluded that there was a cover-up in 1892 by what I call the Spreckels Machine in San Diego to protect John Spreckels (owner of the Hotel Del and of most San Diego infrastructure following the financial crash of the 1880s and the unseating of San Diego's earlier mogul, Connecticut businessman Alonzo Horton.

History clearly indicates that, a few weeks after the Beautiful Stranger perished by a gunshot to the head at the Hotel Del, the Queen of Hawai'i was overthrown by U.S. corporations (Republican Party, Missionary Party, Bayonet Constitution, and other predictable elements in the U.S. rise to the status of a global imperial power in the 1890s). All of that history taken into account, like many very wealthy families, the Spreckelses (headquartered in San Francisco), had their share of scandals including extra-marital affairs. It is entirely possible that John Spreckels might have dallied with a maid whose name was something like Charlotte Barnard (just a guess on my part), which makes the Beautiful Stranger's choice of a fake name (Lottie A. Bernard) all the more logical. The letter A appears in more than one instance within the context of this affair, and I believe it is an effort by Kate Morgan (the sociopathic grifter who dreamed up the sordid blackmail affair) to train her hapless front-woman (Lizzie Wyllie, pregnant and out of luck in unforgivingly cruel Victorian times). Lizzie was a bit of an airhead at times, and needed coaching...all of that and more can be found in the text of my nonfiction analysis *Dead Move.*

Lo and behold then, someone has created a fictional narrative from all this, asserting that a (fake) person named Charlotte Barnard has been identified, in an obvious effort to capitalize on my painstaking work in these volumes.

On a similar note, a troll has created a false narrative about Lizzie Wyllie (the beautiful young woman who actually died at the Hotel Del, not Kate Morgan as falsely reported by the Spreckels Machine coverup). Lizzie was a gorgeous young shopgirl from Detroit, who had dreams of becoming a great stage actress. Witnesses who saw her reported that she was elegant, was stylishly dressed, and displayed the manners of a famous actress. This is entirely different from the homely, dark-eyed Kate Morgan of whom a photograph has survived. And, tragically, from a sketch of the corpse done by a police artist in San Diego, Lizzie's mother was able to identify her daughter as the dead person. In addition, any number of evidentiary items confirm her identity as Lizzie (not Kate Morgan, as the cover-up would have use believe). For example, just to pick one such item, the dead woman was connected with a missing house maid in Los Angeles, named Katie Logan (in whose possessions Los Angeles Police found a travel trunk containing possessions of Kate Morgan and of Lizzie Wyllie). The hotel's official history states that, from evidence gathered in late 1892, the woman in Los Angeles had told a fellow house maid at the L. A. Grant home, where both were employed, that her real name was Lizzie; after which, she quickly corrected herself and told the other maid that she preferred to go by Katie Logan. Read my analysis... too much detail to cover in this preface. Yet consider, while I thoroughly investigated records of Lizzie's home area and family in Detroit, and her employement at a book bindery where she became pregnant out of wedlock by a scoundrel named John Longfield (her foreman in the shop), and read the tragic affirmation by Elizabeth Wyllie that the dead girl was indeed her daughter, some troll has chosen to fabricate a false story that Lizzie returned to Detroit, was married, and lived happily ever after. I researched all that and found no evidence for any such events.

I cover all the details in three books on this subject, which are:

1. *Dead Move: Kate Morgan and the Haunting Mystery of Coronado,* which is a scholarly investigation and is nonfiction; in an abundance of scholarly caution, I released the first edition very briefly in 2008 as historical fiction, until I realized that I was really sure of my facts and conclusions;

2. *Lethal Journey*, a historical novel that serves as good starter to get into the details; it was largely taken from a dramatization contained in the first edition of *Dead Move*;

3. *Coronado Mystery*, which is a duet containing the full text of both *Dead Move* and *Lethal Journey*.

In the years since I wrote these books, my thinking on these matters has deepened and matured in many ways.

For one thing, I find it sad that so many people think of this as a 'ghost story' like a Hallowe'en story. In fact, Lizzie Wyllie is a case study in a leading Victorian literary trope, the Fallen Angel. Most major authors of the age created tragic characters of this nature, best exemplified by Thomas Hardy's great classic novel *Tess of the d'Urbervilles: A Pure Woman Faithfully Presented* (1892). I am working on an article about this, on the theme that Victorian literature required a strong heroine to die (tragically), in order to restore the balance of power in favor of male heroes. This is evident in real life as well, including the tragic deaths of Edgar Allan Poe's wife and cousin Virginia Clemm, whom he married when she was 13, and who died at 24 of tuberculosis. Likewise, there are at least two tragic deaths of young women in the life of U.S. author Henry James, including his beautiful female cousin Mary 'Minnie' Temple, who coincidentally also died of TB at age 24.

The story told in *Dead Move* and *Lethal Journey* (bundled as *Coronado Mystery*) is touched by astounding, disturbing coincidences. Lizzie Wyllie, the Detroit beauty who I believe was the Beautiful Stranger, also died around age 24, although not of tuberculosis but of a gunshot to the head. Several false narratives were spread about to protect hotel owner John Spreckels from rumor and ruin, including that Lizzie was really Kate Morgan, murdered by her gambler husband Tom Morgan. There is, however, zero evidence linking Tom Morgan with events in San Diego. Instead the rogue male figure in the story appears to be John Longfield, the gambler and general creep who was Lizzie's foreman at the book bindery in Detroit, who "ruined" her. Lizzie, carrying a dead baby in her womb, and betrayed on all sides, with nobody left to turn to, is known to have journeyed into San Diego on the last afternoon of her life, barely able to walk any more from those "terrible medicines" noted by Dr. Mertzman, and in a Fifth Avenue shop she bought the gun with which she was about to end her life. Well, I don't want to retell all the detail that I have so carefully and laboriously assembled in good working order for readers. Suffice it to say, I rest my case on the merits of its presentation..

So please, enjoy a rousing story (*Lethal Journey*), delve into a wealth of tantalizing and true historical detail (*Dead Move*), and form your own opinion without being misled by trolls and saboteurs. If anything, I highly recommend reading the Hotel Del Coronado's well-researched, official book on the subject, titled *Beautiful Stranger: The Ghost of Kate Morgan and the Hotel Del Coronado*, while carefully considering the facts presented there, and the conclusions to which they have led me. She was not Kate Morgan, but Lizzie Wyllie. The tragedy of Lizzie Wyllie deserves to be heard, understood, and grieved. Not as a silly and shallow ghost story, but as the true story of a beautiful young woman who got into trouble in a cruel and unforgiving age (Victorian), was betrayed by all those closest to her, and ended up taking her own life during the night of a terrible sea storm that would be remembered as 'the Storm of the Century.'

Thank you, and Happy Reading.

John T. Cullen

San Diego, California

October 2020

Preface to the 2017 Edition of Dead Move

As I go to press with the 125th Anniversary (1892-2017) edition of Dead Move in 2016, I shall confirm that my conclusions over the past decade have affirmed themselves more strongly than ever. By the second edition, I had begun to see the logic of the proposition that John Spreckels had an army of private police working for him undercover. He owned much of San Diego and most of Coronado as the 1890s began, as a way of staking his own territory in the face of his irrepressible German immigrant father (Claus, headquartered in San Francisco), who had built not one but several fortunes over the years. John Spreckels was his father's right-hand man, nonetheless, and when the rival Dole and Missionary corporate interests threatened the Spreckels sugar empire in Hawai'I, John Spreckels helped his father in launching a blitz in defense.

Staunch Spreckels ally King David Kalakaua of Hawai'i had stayed at John Spreckels' newly acquired Hotel del Coronado at Christmas 1890, before traveling north to San Francisco, where the Merrie Monarch (as the enlightened and progressive ruler of sovereign Hawai'i was called) died practically in Claus' arms at the Palace Hotel in January 1891. A cousin of the king took over the monarchy—Queen Liliuokalani, to be overthrown by Spreckels' corporate rivals in January 1893 just weeks after the episode of the Beautiful Stranger at John Spreckels' Hotel del Coronado.

Kate Morgan, 26, marshaled her accomplices to blackmail Spreckels at the worst possible moment—Lizzie Wyllie, 24, and John Longfield, the man who 'ruined' Lizzie by getting her pregnant out of wedlock, despite being a husband and father at home in Detroit. I doubt she understood the macrohistoric context of the Spreckels sugar fortune, the monarchy in Honolulu, the Democratic-Republican rivalry in the United States, the involvement of both President Harrison (a Democrat) and a Republican Congress whose corporate interests ruled the press and won the battle to unlawfully conquer Hawai'i. The politics involving Pineapple King Sanford Dole (soon to be the winner) and Sugar Baron Claus Spreckels extended not only to Washington, D.C., but to London, where HRH Crown Princess Victoria Ka'iulani, in her early 20s, was a student and a guest at the court of Queen Victoria (her namesake).

There can be no doubt that a family like the Spreckelses, and a man like John Spreckels, would surround themselves with security staff on the order of the Pinkertons. There can likewise be no doubt that the Spreckels Machine (as I call it) fended for themselves and their employer in the absence of a real police department, and a credible city government for that matter (city hall and the police headquarters were located in the middle of the Stingaree, one of the West Coast's most notorious red light districts). Spreckels owned the major newspapers in San Diego. While Spreckels was in Washington, D.C., desperately negotiating with President Benjamin Harrison and a hostile Republican Congress, the invisible agents in San Diego were taking care of business. I tend now to think they may have been on to Kate Morgan's blackmail scheme even as Lizzie got off the train at the Santa Fe Depot to begin her short life as the fictitious Lottie A. Bernard. It's odd that she was allowed to sign in at the Hotel del Coronado, counter to strict Victorian rules and morays about reputable women not being allowed to travel without a proper chaperone (usually a male family member, either her husband, a brother, or her father). She was shadowed every moment by an odd bellman named West, who inexplicably glued himself to her. If I had to lay odds, the Spreckels Machine could have arrested Lizzie on the first day—logically, however, they would have used her as bait to try (unsuccessfully) to snare the mastermind, Kate Morgan, who remained painfully out of even Lizzie's reach along with John Longfield, whom one tends to think Kate had appropriated as a bed partner for herself.

When I wrote *Lethal Journey*, the noir period thriller (an 1892 gaslight mystery novel) in 2009, I already had this sinister and dark background in play. I make less of it in *Dead Move*, and more of it in Lethal Journey. The reader who endures the joys and pains of both books will have a far deeper perspective of 1892 San Diego and the Beautiful Stranger affair than most local intellectuals and citizens. I stand by my research and conclusions more strongly than ever.

Preface to the 2012 Third Edition of Dead Move

Time and reflection have only deepened the conclusions I drew in my original, painstaking research that led to the 2008 First and Second Editions of this scholarly, nonfictional analysis of the famous Hotel del Coronado 1892 true crime and ghost story.

The entire enigmatic true crime case was the result of a blackmail attempt against the fabulously wealthy but imperiled John D. Spreckels, scion of a vast Hawai'i based sugar cane fortune. All of what I discovered, and my conclusions from it, have been hidden in plain sight for over 120 years.

There is nothing paranormal, conspiratorial, or invented about the facts as I lay them out. This is, to be sure, a very old, brittle, long-cold police case with missing pieces. As is the case in all history researches, it is amazing how much we know, yet heartbreaking what has been lost. Luckily, a complete, plausible scenario can be deduced from what has come down to us, recorded both in local San Diego sources and in our national histories.

What is new in this Third Edition primarily consists of two things.

❧ 1 ❦

I have replaced the dramatized reenactment of Lottie A. Bernard's life and death at the Hotel del Coronado with the complete text of my dark 1892 thriller Lethal Journey.

Lethal Journey conforms to my historical research, except Tom Morgan is dramatically embellished. These revelations would have been obvious 120+ years ago, with honest, and objective scrutiny.

A historian's dilemma confounds the choice of either narrative. On the one hand, Lethal Journey is fiction, though closely based on true fact. On the other hand, the original dramatization was based on hour by hour, day by day known facts as gathered in the Hotel del Coronado Heritage Department's official book Beautiful Stranger (see Bibliography in End Notes). The problem is one of granularity, for lack of a better way to describe it. Even in the dramatization, I often had to transition from one moment to the next with an imagined gesture or conversation, because we do not have a running film of the dead woman's five final, agonizing days.

The hourly events are pretty well captured in the carefully detailed account of her passage, as recorded mainly in news stories and interviews from the time. To include both the dramatization and Lethal Journey would be redundant. I made a Solomonic choice of Lethal Journey, with only the following caveat.

I have independently concluded that the myths and legends about Kate Morgan's husband, Tom Morgan, have no discernible basis in fact. Their marriage was real, they did lose a baby son (Edward), and they lived in Iowa until their apparent separation for reasons that have nothing to do with this story.

In Lethal Journey (as in the earlier dramatization) I did not entirely cast aside the legend of Tom Morgan as a gambler and, with the publication of an unfortunate book in 1987, possibly a murderer.

In my novel Lethal Journey, written from a noirish screenplay suggested by a play producer, I used the most rousing elements of the legend (Tom Morgan as a violent and dangerous cardsharp), together with my scholarly analysis. Readers are asked simply to remember that the conclusion of Dead Move is that Lizzie most likely committed suicide out of despair and sickness (murder is unlikely, though not 100% ruled out).

❧ 2 ❦

My earlier suspicions of a cover-up have, for me, become firmly entrenched in logic and conviction. The hastily convened and absurdly brief Coroner's Inquest are too blatantly improbable to not have been engineered for purposes of getting things over with, and shielding John D. Spreckels. The forbidding of an autopsy, which would have revealed her pregnancy and thus cast a shadow of doubt on Spreckels, is another blatant factor—in fact, shifting the identity of the victim to Kate Morgan further obfuscated the issue. If the dead woman was not pregnant (as Dr. B. F. Mertzman said she was), then there could be no blackmail. Without a cogent reason for the entire affair, the shadowy issue of blackmail would be permanently covered up. The cover-up is still working quite well to this very day.

The logic for a massive cover-up is impeccable. John Spreckels was the scion of a fabulously wealthy, by then old-money family of the Gilded Age. The better known 'Robber Baron' names (Astor, Vanderbilt, Carnegie, Rockefeller, et al.) were primarily national in character, whereas the stories of John Spreckels and James and Sanford Dole were international. The story of the blackmail at the Hotel del Coronado, therefore, has national and international ramifications. These have been painfully evident all along, but are only now revealed to be firmly linked to global events at the time.

The better known Robber Barons (as historians often call the mega-wealthy U.S. aristocracy of the Gilded Age) derive their pedigree from industries within the vastness of the 48 contiguous states. On pragmatic terms, they acquired vast wealth and tended to marry their daughters to bankrupt but titled British aristocrats to blatantly affirm their loyalties to foreign monarchy rather than the strict anti-monarchist traditions of the U.S. Founding Fathers, and indeed of the British North American colonies (which made the War of Independence possible from a U.S. perspective, within global superpower politics of the late 18th Century). The century-long drive to expand U.S. boundaries west to the Pacific Ocean is called Manifest Destiny. Its racist, sectarian, and related bigotries made an irresistible fuel whose combustion consumed all that stood in its way—be it the Native North American, the Spanish or Russian empires, or the boundaries of sovereign Mexico. The drive westward was all but over by the 1880s.

Without pause, a new class of internationalist power brokers and corporate moguls—e.g., Claus Spreckels, John Spreckels, Sanford Dole, and James Dole (the 'Pineapple King')—continued the Gilded Age's wealth-driven, quasi-religious fervor masked in the slogan of Manifest Destiny, which brooked no opposition.

The 1890 U.S. Census included the declaration that the Frontier was closed. However, expansionary U.S. political, religious, and economic forces pressed on beyond Continental borders. Men like Dole and Spreckels created trans-oceanic fortunes that seem, in retrospect, a continuation of Manifest Destiny by other means.

In the 1840s, it had taken many months, or several years, to laboriously cross the United States on foot or on horseback, via the famous Conestoga Wagons or Prairie Schooners. Just half a century later, the modern person of the 1890s could cross the continent in luxury, in a week or less, aboard the vast arterial and capillary network of the Transcontinental Railroad system.

Likewise, John Spreckels in Washington, D. C. and his father Claus in San Francisco could communicate within hours, coast to coast via telegraph network amid delicate, doomed negotiations over the fate of Hawai'i, and of Spreckels' vast sugar cane plantations.

The telegraph was the 'Internet' of its time, which gave rise to national news coverage by Yellow Press moguls like Joseph Pulitzer and William Randolph Hearst. Scandal, lies, and political-corporate propaganda would be a better term than 'news' for what came out of the Yellow Press. For much of the U.S. public, such coverage was all the exposure they would ever have to national or international events. They had nothing else to go on, so they believed whole-heartedly that the Hawai'ian people were pagan savages deserving of conquest and domination, and that the beautiful, cultured, Anglican-Hawai'ian (and Scottish) Crown Princess Victoria Ka'iulani was a brutal and ugly cannibal with a bone through her nose.

The national scandal of the Beautiful Stranger at the Hotel del Coronado was merely an early dry run for the excesses and propaganda of the Yellow Press. Spreckels' newspapers and agents in Coronado and San Diego succeeded in covering up the worst of his exposure. The Yellow Press relied on half-truths and innuendo to darkly hint of the Beautiful Stranger's alleged liaisons with men in the highest places. In the tightly and cruelly repressed Victorian world, that alone was enough to sell oceans of newsprint to gullible and titillated men and women across the United States.

The Yellow Press' alignment with the corporate-led coup in Honolulu, January 1893, and their defamation of the Hawai'ian people, were prelude to the United States' 1898 acquisition of the Spanish Empire. This is no longer current events, but substantiated and commonly understood history.

The War with Spain came upon a constant drumbeat to war in the Yellow Press, fueled by feverish allegations that an accidental boiler room explosion aboard the U.S.S. Maine in Havana, Cuba Harbor was a deliberate act by Spanish saboteurs. Cuba was a fertile island producing huge quantities of sugar, tobacco, and other goods on the back of an impoverished, near-slave class of human beings who were, due to their race and religion, not covered by the grandiose promises and short deliveries of Manifest Destiny.

❧ 3 ❦

Brief Publication History. I conducted my initial, substantial research on this case in 2006-2008, using my own resources and the Internet, while relying heavily on the excellent groundwork laid by the official Hotel del Coronado Heritage Department historian in their publication Beautiful Stranger: the Ghost of Kate Morgan and the Hotel del Coronado (Heritage Dept., 2002, 2005).

Moving with what proved to be an excess of caution, I initially released the book as a novel of historical fiction. This is a time-honored way of advancing a historical hypothesis. As I soon discovered, this put my research into an unintended limbo between fact and fiction, only in terms of how it was perceived. Within a few weeks, still in 2008, I released the same text in a more boldly stated theory format (nonfiction, history) under the same title, as a 2nd Ed.

In 2009, at the suggestion of an interested play producer from out of state, who had been stationed in Coronado during his Navy days and loved the Hotel Del and the ghost story, I wrote a dark, noirish novel which I published under the title Lethal Journey. The Second Edition of *Dead Move* contained a dramatization of events involving Lizzie Wyllie (the true Beautiful Stranger, who died at the hotel and gave rise to the famous ghost legend). Lethal Journey allowed me to take a few liberties, incorporating the best elements of the legend (cover-up) as received for over a century, along with my careful, scholarly analysis in <u>Dead Move</u>.

In 2012 (120th Anniversary Edition of the Beautiful Stranger's death), bowing to the strong demand for <u>Dead Move</u>, and the fact that <u>Lethal Journey</u> was often lost in the shuffle among the constant outpouring of New York-hyped thrillers, I decided to drop the somewhat creaky and obsolete dramatization from <u>Dead Move</u>, and instead include the full text of Lethal Journey in the current edition that you are reading.

For the 2017 (125th Anniversary Edition) I am retitling the duet as Coronado Mystery, to include both Dead Move and Lethal Journey. Each of those two books also is to appear separately to offer more choices to interested readers. See <u>www.coronadomystery.com</u>.

End Notes for Dead Move

[1] *Beautiful Stranger: The Ghost of Kate Morgan and the Hotel del Coronado*, ISBN 978-0916251737 available in the gift shop, in most San Diego area bookstores, and online.

[2] Official Hotel del Coronado website—www.hoteldel.com/

[3] In competition with at least one other famous, disputed legend—that in 1920, the visiting Prince of Wales (one day King Edward VIII) met his future wife, Wallis Simpson, at the hotel while she was living in Coronado as the wife of a young U.S. Navy officer stationed a mile away at North Island. That legend now debunked.

[4] San Diego Historical Society website

[5] HD28MR (notation convention: Heritage Dept. book, page 28, middle right)

[6] Photo: http://www.sandiegohistory.org/journal/56april/images/page19.jpg Article: http://www.sandiegohistory.org/journal/56april/palace.htm

[7] SD Historical Society, http://www.sandiegohistory.org/journal/56july/cattle.htm

[8] *History of San Diego 1542-1908* by William Smythe, San Diego Historical Society, http://www.sandiegohistory.org/books/smythe/7-4.htm

[9] More info about the peninsula is in the Maps section at book's end

[10] HD7UL (Heritage Dept. page 7, upper left)

[11] HD8LL (Heritage Dept. page 8, lower left)

[12] HD54 (Heritage Dept. entire page 54)

[13] HD54

[14] HD8

[15] HD42UR

[16] HD24UL

[17] In those days, San Diego's numbered streets were streets. Today, from 1st to 12th, they are avenues. Starting with 13th, they are still today streets.

[18] D Avenue was today's Broadway. Yesteryear's lettered avenues are today's lettered streets.

[19] HD11

[20] http://www.measuringworth.com/uscompare/ estimates $571.43 using the Consumer Price Index as a measure to compare 1892 and 2007 (115 years).

[21] HD12LL

[22] HD 63LL

[23] HD 39LR.

[24] In 1892, the Coronado Beach as we know it in the 2000s had not yet been created, and the hotel sat very close to the ocean.

[25] Probably a typical example of imaginative reasoning and inaccurate reporting. At the inquest, Cone says there was blood on the step [HD18UR]. The gardener Koeppen also saw blood [HD20ML]. Deputy Coroner Stetson saw blood around

and underneath the gun [HD34LL].See Part 3, Day 1, in this book for a conjecture on how blood could have gotten there after being washed away by a fierce rain storm.

[26] At the inquest, Deputy Coroner Stetson describes it as a 'valise' [HD34RM]

[27] HD40-41

[28] While Frank Heath did not know where she went from his shop [HD22LL], W. P. Walters, witness in Chick's Gun Shop, said he saw her leave to go to the Combination, another retail store, which sounds like a clothing store, and we know she was 'well-dressed' and seemed to like clothing. It seems odd that a depressed woman about to commit suicide, who could hardly walk, would saunter around town looking at clothes. Walters says (he was told by another man) she also went across the street to Schiller & Murtha's dry good store. Walters watched her for a time. [HD33LL-HD33UR].

[29] HD41UL

[30] Stetson testified at the inquest on the previous day that there were handkerchiefs with an unreadable name embroidered, which thought might be "Little Anderson." [HD34LR].

[31] HD29RM.

[32] HD42UL

[33] HD42LL

[34] HD71-72

[35] HD43

[36] HD74UL

[37] *Chronological List of San Diego City Officials*, San Diego Historical Society website.

[38] University of Iowa, http://sdrc.lib.uiowa.edu/lucile/publishers/winn/WINN.HTM

[39] HD69-70

[40] HD73

[41] HD45-46

[42] HD73-74

[43] HD46-47.

[44] HD74UR

[45] HD47-48

[46] HD65-66

[47] HD73

[48] HD48-49

[49] HD66-67

[50] HD70-71

[51] HD75

[52] HD49-50

[53] HD50

[54] HD50

[55] HD67-68

[56] HD51

[57] HD68-69

[58] A baffling observation that clearly seems to be an alibi—either to cover why the couple are not together, or to cover why Tom is not at home in Iowa. Why, if Victorians frowned on women traveling alone, did her uncle not question this?

[59] Those relatives could not identify the body one way or another. They had not seen her since she was a small child, so relatives from Pasadena were supposed to come to identify the body—but there is no record they ever showed up. Had Lizzie Wyllie (the first i.d. on the body after the Lottie A. Bernard persona became suspect) been alive, there can be absolutely no doubt the police would have found her, or she would have notified police she was alive. This strongly supports the notion that Lizzie was in fact dead, which makes her, *de facto,* the strongest candidate for the role of the dead woman at the Hotel del Coronado.

[60] 35HDLL

[61] It was extremely dangerous for anyone to travel alone in that era. Consider the thousands of innocent men shanghaied in the bars of Portland, Oregon in those days alone. And if a woman was raped, Victorians regarded her as a 'fallen woman'—so, society protected her not only from rape, but from social stigma.

[62] This housekeeper, in another wild urban legend connected to the saga) is said to have committed suicide in the "heavily haunted" Room 3519, not the same as Lottie Bernard/Lizzie's Room 3327. (Room numbers were different then, and Lizzie's room was 302.)

[63] HD24UL

[64] HD29UR

[65] HD11

[66] HD12LL

[67] HD46UR

[68] HD36

[69] HD42LL

[70] http://www.mchsmuseum.com/clausspreckels.html Monterey County Historical Society website

[71] *Encyclopedia of San Francisco*: http://www.sfhistoryencyclopedia.com/

[72] HD69-70

[73] HD73

[74] HD73LL

[75] HD45-46

[76] HD46LL-UR

[77] HD73-74

[78] HD46-47

[79] HD74UR

[80] HD47-48

[81] HD65-66

[82] HD48-49

[83] HD70

[84] HD49-50

[85] HD50

[86] HD50
[87] http://en.wikipedia.org/wiki/Embalming
[88] http://en.wikipedia.org/wiki/Embalming
[89] BS34LL
[90] HD54
[91] HD2UR
[92] HD54
[93] HD43LL
[94] HC43LL
[95] HD66UL
[96] HD42LL
[97] HD41-42 Interviewed by *The San Diego Union*, Dec. 1, the unnamed doctor is almost certainly B. F. Mertzman, given that he repeats statements attributed to Mertzman (e.g., it being ridiculous to think she had cancer, but most likely show herself while pregnant, abandoned, and in a lovers' spat.)
[98] HD27UL
[99] *The Stingray* by Russell, Findlay, posted by Cal Tech Library (http://calteches.library.caltech.edu/149/01/Russell.pdf)
[100] HD28LR
[101] HD70ML, HD68UR
[102] HD74LL
[103] http://en.wikipedia.org/wiki/Dickens#Characters
[104] http://en.wikipedia.org/wiki/Pre-Raphaelite_Brotherhood
[105] http://en.wikipedia.org/wiki/Ophelia_%28painting%29
[106] http://en.wikipedia.org/wiki/Ophelia_%28character%29
[107] http://en.wikipedia.org/wiki/Hard_Times
[108] Official San Diego City website, Police Department history, www.sandiego.gov/police/
[109] HD15UL
[110] HD36
[111] HD 47L